The Education of Little Homo Sapiens

Human Evolution and the Intelligent Design of School

Steven Welliever

The Education of Little Homo Sapiens
Human Evolution and the Intelligent Design of School

Steven Welliever

Edited by Jessica Archer

ISBN-10: 1491050853
ISBN-13: 978-1491050859

DEDICATION

This book is dedicated to my boys Desi and Gus, and all school kids – present, past, and future.

CONTENTS

PREFACE

Preface

Nothing in Education Makes Sense Except in the Light of Evolution

"In order to change an existing paradigm you do not struggle to try and change the problematic model. You create a new model and make the old one obsolete."

— R. Buckminster Fuller.

Years ago I was doodling on some graph paper waiting for a faculty meeting to begin. Most of the teachers were sitting around tables that were all shoved together into a large rectangle, except for one of my colleagues who was way over in the corner squatting on the floor. Something looked out of place. I discretely asked what was up. She explained that humans didn't evolve to sit on chairs – they were a recent cultural invention. If I remember correctly, she may have been dealing with some back pain problems. That chair comment was unexpected but logical. I suddenly began a paranoid estimation of how many hours in my life I had spent sitting in a chair. A dark realization crept over me: This whole place we call 'school' was like that – a terrible fit for our evolutionary biology. Un-human... Inhumane! Who could start a faculty meeting at a time like this? I have pursued this thought ever since – Does our school culture compliment our human biology, or are they at odds? More importantly, how much does this affect learning?

In 1973, Theodosius Dobzhansky published an essay in *American Biology Teacher* with the oft-repeated title, "Nothing in Biology Makes Sense Except in the Light of Evolution." The article advocated for making evolution the central theme of biology education. "Without that light," he added, "it becomes a pile of sundry facts some of them interesting or curious but making no meaningful picture as a whole." There is no denying the explanatory power and coherence that evolution has given the field of biology. I suspected that Dobzhansky's central theme would reveal something that would make sense of the school world.

In the classroom, the fact that humans are a biological species that is the product of ongoing evolution seems to have escaped us. From an evolutionary point of view, schools are rife with bad practices. The problems are so ubiquitous and the public model of schooling is so homogeneous that they don't appear to be problems: they are widely accepted norms. When we take so much of modern school culture for granted, many of the incompatibilities with our biology create unnecessary barriers to learning that have become hidden in plain sight.

I decided to take Dobzhansky's idea that evolution is biology's central organizing theme and apply it to our education system – a system that presently might be called *The Mis-Education of Little Homo Sapiens*. Once we take the time to learn about ourselves as a species, designing a functional educational system should fall into place rather easily.

I use the lens of modern science to look back through the rear-view mirror of human evolution to find solutions to the most intractable problems facing schools today. I propose that the more central a trait is to our humanity, the more important of a variable it will be in the success of the educational process. This approach makes for a truly universal human education framework that can adapt to fit most any curriculum, environment, setting, culture, or population. This is because it works on the deepest level – our common hard-wired biology.

I dubbed the philosophy 'Paleopedagogy': Paleo [pā'lē-ō] old, ancient, or prehistoric | pedagogy ['pe-də- gō-jē] the art or science of teaching. It is both predictive and prescriptive – and powerfully so. In other words, you can use the framework to identify problems and illuminate solutions.

The school reform movement has created pointless and divisive debates about teacher accountability, standardized testing, achievement gaps, and more. Our attempts to improve the education system have revolved around trying to decipher what does and doesn't work, largely based on what little variation has existed over the past century. Most proposed reforms are cosmetic and desperate fixes that fail to address the most challenging problems. Some hold a romantic notion that schooling worked better in the past, and it can again, if we could only get tough about it. Some frustrated parents think perhaps it is time to blow up the whole paradigm of school and start over from scratch- or even forgo 'school' altogether. As we flounder between common-core standards, charter schools, private schools, home-schooling, un-schooling, and more, it's worth asking "What if the common aspects of our schooling system are simply out of sync with our humanity?"

Anatomically modern *Homo sapiens* have been around for at least 100,000 years – and schools for only recent generations. Our ancient hunting and gathering ancestors were mentally capable of the same things that we do today. Put a different way, we still have ancient, small-scale, social, hunter-gatherer brains that desperately need a fitting environment in which to thrive.

Our education system is in desperate need of reinvention. I propose one that will not only be relevant for the 21st century, but will likely be just as logical 50,000 years in the future as it would have been 50,000 years in the past. So, ready or not, here it comes – the school reform reasoning you haven't heard yet. It is time to shed some light on the subject of education… and, this time it is going to make sense. Nothing in Education Makes Sense Except in the Light of Evolution!

** Note:

Throughout this text, Little Homo Sapiens is being used as the proper name of an imaginary student, and so the name will appear with the species name *sapiens* capitalized as Sapiens. The Latin *Genus* and *species* name for us humans, *Homo sapiens*, also appears in the text, in its traditional form. Additionally, do not be confused, as Little Homo Sapiens will change ages, genders, special-needs, and other demographic backgrounds throughout the text.

PART I

No Student is an Island

CHAPTER 1

Our Web Of Relationships

At some point in our Stone Age past, human beings began to do something so incredible that it would forever separate us from the rest of the animal kingdom: we began to speak. This markedly human trait likely evolved for the grand purpose of socializing with one another. Speaking allowed us to expand our social networks, which increased our safety and security. In short, socializing isn't just a small aspect of being human. It is what makes us human – and allows us to thrive.

But consider our social nature in the context of schools. A common conversation during parent-teacher conferences might bluntly be interpreted like this: "Your daughter's main academic problem is that she socializes too much." While chatting in class may often be incompatible with today's classroom, the student is doing exactly what she evolved to do. Historically, in an evolutionary sense, this is the hallmark of a successful human being. In this chapter, I will briefly cover the science that surrounds discussions about our social nature at school.

The Social Brain Theory (Dunbar, 1998), championed by Oxford evolutionary psychology professor Robin Dunbar, is a leading explanation for the evolution of the human brain. Our large neocortex (the outer layer of brain) anatomically sets our brains apart from our primate cousins due to its size and more recent evolution. His research suggests that all of this 'socializing' was actually the driving force behind the brain's evolution. Our large brains are an evolutionary adaptation for being social, and for managing a large network of friends and family.

The qualities that have given humans an evolutionary

advantage throughout our history will continue to be beneficial. It is time to start viewing our evolutionary strengths as our strengths in the classroom, starting with the traits that have made us successful humans in the first place. Little Homo Sapiens is first and foremost a social being. Therefore our evolutionary social biology will be the first stone we turn over to look for problems and to reveal remedies.

Hierarchy of Social Groups

Once we've accepted that schools are indeed a social endeavor, we must consider what it means to be social – what it means to be a 'friend'. Adults may have a range of relationships from the very close 'emergency contact' family member to the neighbor you might offer surplus garden zucchini. But is there a pattern to all of this?

Research on human group sizes finds that we typically network in groups of specific, predictable sizes. Researchers analyzed data sets of human group sizes and searched for a pattern. They discovered that there is order to be found in social group sizes as illustrated in Table 1 (Zhou, et al 2005). The group sizes are discrete in the sense that the sizes cluster tightly around specific values. Increasingly larger group size can be imagined as concentric rings, like ripples from a stone thrown in a pond. You are in the center, your closest inner circle of friends and family come next, and so on to rings of consecutively more distant relationships. This table will be a fundamental theme running throughout the book and will guide us in configuring schools.

Table 1. Human Social Group Sizes
(Adapted from Discrete Hierarchical Organization of Social Group Sizes Zhou, W-X, D Sornette, RA Hill and RIM Dunbar (2005) Proc. R. Soc. B 272:439-444)

Human Social Group Sizes (Adapted from Zhou, et al, 2005)			
Group	AVG Size	Description	Range
Individual	1	Yourself	1
Support Clique	4.6	Highest source of support; turn to when suffering or financially broke	3-5
Sympathy Group	14.3	Share special ties, frequent (monthly) contact	12-20
Band	42.6	Drawn from cognitive group (somewhat unstable)	30-50
Cognitive Group	132.5	All the people you can know and maintain relationships with	150-ish
Mega-band	566	Larger social unit	~500
Tribe	1728	Linguistic group	1000 – 2000

Do you notice something interesting about these numbers? Researchers discovered that the group sizes seemed to scale at a ratio a little larger than 3 (as shown in Figure 1) (Zhou, et al, 2005). Each group size can be multiplied by about 3 to reach the next group size. In short, 3 is the magic number.

Figure 1. Human group sizes scale at an average ratio of 1:3.3 (Data from Zhou, et al, 2005). Each successively larger ring contains all of the relationships of the rings inside.

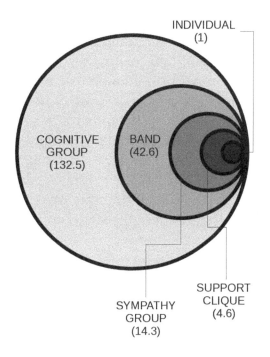

This phenomenon is called discrete scale invariance (Sornette, 1998). The fractal analysis used to uncover this social pattern has also helped to explain things as varied as earthquakes, branching patterns in your lungs, and stock market behavior. Here, the fractal dimension, or 'zoom level' is the same between each successive group size – a little over 3 on average. This scaling ratio is a beautiful part of the geometry of our social biology. A numerical pattern this innate commands respect: don't mess with something as intrinsic as this! This is a natural pattern that must be worked with, not against, for efficiency and effectiveness.

Dunbar's Number: The outer limits of social networks

In the era of digital social media, the term 'friend' itself has been co-opted and commoditized by clicks. It is time to take stock of all of our relationships, digital or otherwise, and ask the question: How many of these 'friends' would do a small favor for me? Is there an outer limit to our social networks?

In 1992, Robin Dunbar noticed a pattern among various social primate species (chimps, monkeys, orangutans, etc.) He noticed a relationship between the maximum social group size found in each primate species and the size of an outer layer of their brains (Dunbar, 1992). Dunbar found that as this outer 'neocortex' layer increased size, the primates' maximum social group sizes increased as well. Using this correlation, Dunbar was able to predict the extent of the social sphere of the most social primate of them all – humans. This number is commonly called Dunbar's Number; it is an estimation of the cognitive group size, the extent of an individual's personal relationships. His estimate was around 150 people. This is the brain's outer limit – all the people that you can truly know and maintain a relationship with.

'Dunbar's Number' is supported consistently in research. Groups of this size are observed in ancient and modern human cultures around the globe. I took a quick break while writing this chapter and went for a jog through Columbia-River-irrigated-Eastern-Washington where signs of the cognitive group were literally all around. A historical marker mentions that Nez Perce leader Chief Joseph was forcibly exiled here to the Colville Reservation, with about "150" of his people. Further down the highway, a Hutterite farming community outside of Odessa, WA splits into daughter colonies around this number. But what happens when you exceed Dunbar's Number? Certainly we all 'know of' more than 150 people. Once you reach the outer limit, your brain simply doesn't have the time or the power to know those people as individuals. At this point, the brain begins to group into 'types' of people (Dunbar, 1996). Little Homo Sapiens ceases to be an individual;

Little Homo Sapiens becomes a type.

Starting with this cognitive group figure of around 150, we will now spend the next chapters fleshing out the significance of the hierarchy of human social group sizes at school.

CHAPTER 2

School Size: Acknowledging our cognitive limits

When living in times of rapid technological advancement on a planet with 7+ billion people, it is sobering to come to grips with a very finite human limitation. There is an outer bound to the radius of our social circles. A limit we must reckon with. But what does it mean for schools that have hundreds, or sometimes even thousands of students? I want to discuss overall school size before the often lamented issue of class size. It is at the overall school size where we cross the line of the cognitive group maximum. This is the threshold between interpersonal knowledge and 'random kid who is a certain flavor of background noise'.

In my home state of Washington, it is typical to have 30 students in a high school class. Commonly, teachers have 5 class periods of instruction, with an additional period set aside for planning. Suddenly, we have reached Dunbar's Number. The result is that the number of students a teacher encounters on a given school day often exceeds the cognitive limit of the number of people a human can possibly know. Likewise for students; they can have more classmates than they can possible know.

Individualizing Instruction

When students cease to be individuals, some teaching techniques commonly touted in our school system lose their potential. One example of this is the use of 'differentiation' in the classroom. Differentiated instruction is educational jargon for:

"an instructional technique that includes various ways to teach content and assess learning. It is used to meet student needs and differences in readiness, interests, and learning styles."

– Family Dictionary of Education Terms, 2nd Edition 2010-2011, Washington State Education Ombudsman, Office of the Governor

In general, differentiation attempts to better accommodate the diversity of students' individual learning needs.

However, knowing a student's unique neurological wiring becomes practically impossible at a scale that exceeds the cognitive group. This fact of human biology pretty much pokes a hole in using differentiation to its potential. Customized instruction can be better practiced in small school environments. Students can be known, especially over a few years, truly as individuals. This depth of understanding of individual student learning preferences would be difficult with group sizes typical of many public schools. Despite the availability of increasing mounds of individual testing and diagnostic data, adequate knowledge of students as individual learners can still be lacking.

Types

Let's further explore the dangers of exceeding the cognitive group size in the school environment by exploring stereotype. As I've mentioned, once you've exceeded the cognitive limit of 150 people, the student brain has no choice but to deal with types of people: Cafeteria Manager, Bus Driver, Principal, Teacher, Coach, Custodian, Office Staff, Nurse, Police Officer...

While stereotyping is reputed as an unreliable and negative habit of mind, it is time for a closer examination. Stereotypes are simply a default framework for knowing how to interact with different kinds of people in a populated setting, a coping mechanism for existing outside of our hunter-gatherer group sizes (Dunbar, 1996).

Now, what does exceeding the cognitive group size look like from the teacher's point of view? What categorical types does a teacher see among the students? Do teachers break down student stereotypes by race and ethnicity, language, gender, socio-economic status, special education status, achievement level, or who knows what? Yes, we all know that in an ideal world, teachers are nice, caring people who will treat everybody as an individual. We know that is what teachers want to do. But the world of school is not an ideal one. Teachers cannot defy the limitations of their own humanity any more than they can defy gravity. We must have the courage to address this question if we are to continue with such large group sizes in our educational environs. When a sea of individuals becomes a school full of types, large school sizes may be inadvertently setting the stage to reinforce achievement gaps according to prevailing academic stereotypes.

Control

Another unfortunate outcome of large school sizes (as a whole, and in terms of class size) is that discipline becomes a core aspect of learning. I reside in Olympia, the state capital of Washington, where the local public schools are ranked among the best in the state. Even at such 'good' schools, the measure of friction in the system resulting from large school sizes is immediately apparent. 'Orientation Night' at the local high school comes across as an introduction to the discipline system rather than an introduction to an educational institution. Even at the fall curriculum night in my 1st grader's class, the 'curriculum' presented was almost exclusively the disciplinary routines. So even in a relatively coveted school district, the amount of discipline and control exerted on the average kid just to maintain such an environment is paramount. What is gained in keeping order comes at a cost. The depth and quality of the learning experience is ultimately adversely affected. We must look at school factors which allow their rich academic programs to take center-stage, and not the discipline routines. Such discipline can in turn be pro-active, prescriptive, personalized, and positive.

Cognitive Group Conclusion

We have compounded a short list of issues generated by school populations greater than the cognitive group size: default to stereotype, lack of individual knowledge in order to customize instruction, a discipline-obsessed system, as well as a lack of social cohesion, interpersonal knowledge, and trust – all which hinder learning.

For a social brain, a room full of unknowns can create anxiety and invisible barriers to learning. When students and teachers cease to know each other as individuals by exceeding the cognitive group size, the fallout is a low-trust atmosphere ripe for stereotype, poor communication, and a heavy reliance on discipline.

I argue that the total number of students and faculty in a school (or functional subunit of a school) should reflect the cognitive group size of around 150 as an upper bound. I believe this is especially true during ages of social development and sensitivity, such as early elementary and middle school years. This allows the maximum number of individuals to have the capacity to be known, beyond stereotype, and to truly have a more personalized educational experience. Each person can be recognized for their individual identity, where the voice of each individual carries significance. All the while, students can reap the benefits of social learning to the maximum extent in a safer, more connected, social environment where efficient communication can take place.

For the same advantageous reasons that humans evolved to be social in the first place, education too should be a social endeavor. If we ignore group size, the consequences are real. In the next few chapters, we will dial in the frequencies of smaller school group sizes using the 'magic' scaling ratio of roughly 3. So, now that Little Homo Sapiens has made it through the school doors, it's time for him to head into class.

CHAPTER 3

Class Size: The dysfunctional army platoon

After standardized testing, class size is probably the most controversial topic in the education world. Here in Washington State, voters have twice posed initiatives to reduce class size – both times without a funding source, Initiatives 728 (2000) and 1351 (2014). Additionally, K-3 class sizes were to be capped at 17 under the first phase of the state Supreme Court's *McCleary v. State of Washington* (2012) school-funding decision, but we're still waiting to see that on the ground. The conversation is increasingly political. But what does science tell us? Does nature have a recipe for class size?

The class size debate typically points back to a hallmark research study called the Tennessee STAR (Student Teacher Achievement Ratio) Study. STAR was a large study in the mid-1980's comparing the success of students in small classes (13-17 kids) to the success of students in large classes (22-25 kids). The study was only for the early grades (K-3). Students in the smaller classes performed significantly better than their peers in the larger classes – not just in the early grades, but throughout their academic careers. These small class sizes provided an even larger benefit to students who were demographically at the bottom of the achievement gap, such as black and low-income students. When students went on to take college entrance exams, the black-white achievement gap was reduced by more than half for students who were in the smaller class sizes.... in kindergarten. A follow-up economic study on the long term benefits of this class size reduction in the early elementary years revealed a 5.5% rate of return (Krueger & Whitmore 2000).

But, is it just a matter of reducing the class size? Or, is there something special about the particular small class sizes used in the STAR study? The issue of class size periodically comes to the forefront of education policy discussion, but never from an evolutionary point of view.

There is one glaring hallmark of the public school class size: it does not fit in any of the categories shown in the hierarchy of human social group sizes (Table 1). In my home state of Washington, class sizes of approximately 30, even in 'good' districts, are typically the norm in middle and high schools. My own kindergartner's class fluctuated in the high 20's. Classes of this size are much too large for a sympathy group, and at the low-end of the range for a band. The public school class size is like that spot in between stations on your radio, where the frequency delivers nothing but static with intermittent garbled hints of nearby frequencies. However, whether you dial in the lower frequency or the higher one may result in a huge difference as to what type of educational experience you can possibly expect to deliver.

The small class sizes used in the Tennessee STAR study fit within the sympathy group size (Table 1). Your sympathy group is composed of around 15 people with whom you share special ties. You may only see these people monthly, but they are your close network. These are the friends or family who you might celebrate an important milestone, birthday, or life event with. Most importantly, your sympathy group is composed of the people with whom you can truly be yourself – these are the people you trust. In an educational setting, where students are exposing their skills and knowledge on a daily basis, trust is critical to success. For this reason, a class size that mirrors the sympathy group size of about 15 is the ideal.

As I mentioned earlier, there are numerous consequences of exceeding the cognitive group size at the school level: default to stereotype, lack of individual knowledge in order to customize instruction, a discipline-obsessed system; and a lack of social cohesion, interpersonal knowledge, and trust that hinders learning. These factors are all at play in the classroom of a large overall school size. And when we exceed the sympathy group size in the classroom, we bring in another layer of educational handicap – an orientation towards rote-learning.

Robin Dunbar remarks in his book *Grooming, Gossip and the Evolution of Language* (1996) that limits to how many people can converse at once is a profound problem for larger classes. There must be strict rules about who can speak when and for what purpose in order to curtail cafeteria-level chaos from ensuing. This drives, or even limits, instructional style to teacher-directed, rote-memorization and away from critical thinking. This is hardly the type of education needed to prepare our youth for the complex problems, changes, and challenges facing society in the 21st century.

Independent Schools

The debate on class sizes seems largely to be one reserved for the sphere of public education. Let's take a look at what's going on in independent schools. Independent schools are state-accredited private schools that are independently governed. The National Association of Independent Schools (NAIS, 2012) reports a median class size of 16. The class size preference found in independent schools is consistent from year-to-year, across grade levels and across geographic regions of the United States. In other words, for schools that can choose their ideal class size, they invariably choose a class fitting a sympathy group. In fact, the most elite independent schools in the United States have a special oval-shaped table in their classrooms, called a Harkness Table, that only fits about 15 kids. Hand-raising is not allowed, or even necessary, during the 'give and take' instructional style that is associated with these tables.

Independent schools have figured out a more optimal scale at which to operate classrooms. The sympathy group class size is maintained with high fidelity across independent schools, even ones that vary widely in mission and philosophy. But independent schools are not the only place to observe patterning consistent with natural human social group sizes.

Platoon

Sympathy group sizes can be seen in other arenas as well. In football, only 11 players are allowed on the field at one time. NBA Basketball teams have a maximum of 15 players on the roster, although only 12 can suit-up for the game. There is no doubt that trust, interpersonal knowledge, and efficient communication is important on the court and on the field, but there is one place where trusting your companions can be a matter of life or death – in war. It is certainly easier to 'read the mind' of somebody you know well.

The size of a military squad fits the sympathy group size. Not only that, but each army unit (squad, platoon, company, and so on) reflects each of the natural human group sizes and scales at a similar ratio. It seems likely that the military has evolved to resemble these natural group sizes – sizes that result in the most 'success'. Scientists have used this comparison to support the phenomenon of a hierarchy of discrete human social group sizes.

"Could it be that the army's structures have evolved so as to mimic the natural hierarchical groupings of everyday social structures, thereby optimizing the cognitive processing of within-group interactions?"

--Zhou, et al, (2005)

Our public schools are one place that have not yet evolved to mimic natural human social group sizes. To make this point, I would like to conduct a brief thought experiment comparing an army platoon to a public school classroom. These groups contain approximately the same number of individuals, but differ dramatically in their organizational substructure.

Lets compare a class size of 30 kids to a military platoon (Figure 2). A platoon consists of 2 to 4 squads; each squad is comprised of ~10 soldiers. A platoon is usually led by a lieutenant with a lower ranking sergeant as second-in-command. Each squad in turn has a leader. Platoons break down into squads in order to get things done. A platoon can accomplish multiple tasks at once through the coordination of squads, who can work in support of each other on more complicated jobs (US Department of the Army, 2004).

Figure 2. Comparing a military platoon and school class of 30 students.

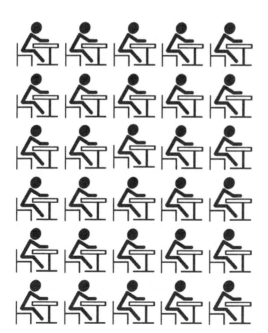

What if we had to tell all of the platoon leaders that they no longer had a second-in-command? And, somehow due to budget cuts, squad leaders will be laid off, which also means squads will no longer exist as functional units. The army could only break down so far as the platoon level, and the lieutenant alone was now directly supervising the entire platoon. The lieutenant now must give directions to everybody in the platoon all at once – even if the information is only relevant to a few soldiers. We won't tell them about the fund-raisers they will need to hold in order to buy gear until later.

Now what are the platoon's chances for success during an actual military operation? Imagine the disruption of communication, coordination, interpersonal issues, and processing challenges created when a single leader is now responsible for such a large set of people.

If we view our public school class as a military platoon, its organizational deficits become obvious. With a class the size of a platoon, discipline and rote learning are crucial just to maintain order. Sadly, many of the benefits of social learning are lost. Thinking about classrooms from this analogous point of view can give us some deep insights.

We simply cannot flaunt millions of years of evolution with a class size of 30+ and expect great results. Little Homo Sapiens deserves better.

Solutions

We must find the courage to fund small class sizes. Priorities for class size reductions should target early elementary school, as well as the middle school years. As we discussed, existing research shows that smaller class sizes in the early years can result in benefits throughout a student's academic career and increase future earnings. Reducing class sizes during the early years, as well as in middle school, allows for social skills to be practiced and learned at a more human scale when it is most pertinent.

You may be wondering, 'What options exist for teachers who want to reap these benefits now?' 'What if I don't want to wait for the political powers in charge to get their act together?'

If large classes are a must, the teacher may consider creating an additional level of organization in the classroom to mimic our naturally evolved social sizes. While teachers commonly use small groups in class, our goal is to create groups that also mirror the intermediate sized 'sympathy group' or 'squad.' The teacher may make use of whatever additional tier of leadership is available, be it student leaders, para-educators, classroom aids, parent volunteers, etc. Targeting instruction to a few different abilities, needs, or particular function might create the opportunity for this level of organization. Split grade-level classes, such as a 3rd/4th grade combination class are often a good place to examine such organizational substructure at work. While additional preparations are taxing for the teacher, classes that make effective use of intermediate-sized groupings sometimes have a hidden strength that can be harnessed. This is nature-patterning – we are mimicking evolution's solutions to design more efficient human systems.

Remember when I said that group sizes determine the quality of the educational program you can expect to deliver? If you have a class of 15, and you are still working it like a class of 30, then there are some missed opportunities at hand. Class size reductions should also be accompanied by instructional technique shifts. Teachers are not often trained or experienced to implement the type of program that can enhance the outcomes of small class sizes. This is especially true after No Child Left Behind federal testing requirements reduced the educational experience to the most basic fundamentals of reading and math. By reducing class size, we provide the opportunity for greater complexity and depth of learning. We also allow for more critical discussions. The structure can facilitate a more democratic environment. Smaller classes allow students the capacity to learn by doing – and as a truly social endeavor. After all, the squad is the military grouping where things get done! Little Homo Sapiens needs an appropriate-scaled classroom environment to thrive just as a soldier needs a squad grouping.

CHAPTER 4

Making Middle School Count: A return to small-scale hunter-gatherer society

No stage of schooling is more universally loathed than the awkward middle school years. Kids starting middle school enter a larger school with many new faces – and this adjustment could not come at a worse time. I like to compare the rate and amount of change that takes place biologically and socially during the middle school years to that of the first three years of life. A larger school combined with social and biological changes can create a perfect storm that suddenly shifts a student's trajectory in school.

Middle school is a time of quickly transitioning toward independence. It is a time when youth look, for perhaps the first time, primarily outward to their reflection from peers for their identity. Where do I fit in? What do I look like to others? Part of that identity is determining - 'What is my identity as a learner'? How a student answers this question influences their progress through high school and beyond.

Environments that promote a positive image as a learner and provide social-emotional support to develop this image are crucial at this stage. Otherwise, as is often the case, this is the inflection point for a downward trajectory for the rest of schooling. The social sensitivity of the middle school years is of paramount priority. This is again where human social group sizes become a critical factor in the design of schooling. The data are in, and middle school lives up to it's nefarious reputation on a spreadsheet.

Comparing Adolescents in K-8 with Middle School

Research from Columbia University (Rockoff and Lockwood, 2010) compared the success of kids attending K-8 model schools (kindergarten through 8th grade) with those attending middle schools. They found a significant difference in the performance of kids in these different settings. Data from New York City showed that middle school attendees suffered a significant drop in math and English scores compared with their adolescent peers from the same grade levels in K-8 settings. The decline was about a .15 standard deviation drop in their math test scores.

Even worse, research shows that middle school becomes the inflection point for a lackluster academic trajectory in relation to their peers in K-8 settings. In a similar study from Florida in 2011 (Schwerdt and West, 2012), middle schoolers whose test scores were tracked into high school were sadly unable to make up for the performance deficits suffered in middle school. The lower achieving half of students were hit the hardest. They fell twice as far as their higher achieving classmates. This disproportionate handicap to achievement gap populations is a tell-tale symptom of a deep school/evolutionary biology conflict. Simply attending a school with a middle school configuration results in academic injury. There is something in the numbers.

To put a qualitative face on this scrutiny of middle schools, Rockoff and Lockwood (2010) looked at parent and student surveys from New York. The surveys confirmed higher ratings for academic rigor, safety, and course offerings for adolescents in K-8 schools compared with their middle school counterparts. It is also noteworthy that they discovered that K-8 students were absent 2 fewer days per year.

What is it about the middle school model that is impacting achievement? Part of the answer lies in the large increase in grade level cohort size. Between school size and class size, there is an intermediate grouping that is not often the focus of attention. Education researchers refer to it as grade level cohort, or all of the kids at a school that are in the same grade level; for example: all of the 5th graders at Mountain View Elementary School, regardless if they are in Mr. A or Miss Z's 5th grade class. Because most middle schools draw attendance from multiple elementary schools, middle schools typically have a much larger grade level cohort size. In the study of New York City schools (Rockoff and Lockwood, 2010), K-8 schools had an average grade level cohort size of 75 and K-5 and K-6 elementary schools had 100 in each grade. In contrast, the middle schools in the study averaged a whopping 200+ students per grade level. The researchers determined that a decent portion of the students' under-performance (about 25%) could be attributed to this increase in grade level cohort size. Too many middle schoolers in one place appears to be a small but noteworthy handicap to academic achievement.

Middle schools mix together a large number of kids who have never met one another. This environment of unfamiliarity can result in anxiety and stress that create significant, invisible impediments to learning that can persist as long as they are in that environment. Trust and emotional safety are important environmental components to the inherent risks in learning. A trusting environment is simply not possible in a large school, due to the aforementioned cognitive limitations. The students' social brains are maxed-out and stifled in this setting; an academic and social paralysis by analysis. The effects of stress, fear and anxiety on learning have been well-documented. However, we haven't done a great job of pinning it on large group size.

You may be wondering – why not just go with a K-8 model? Middle schoolers are not elementary students, and really should not be lumped together with them. Middle school students have a special set of social, emotional, academic, and physical activity needs. Proponents of middle school would argue that they require a program and environment that serves the unique characteristics of the age group. Perhaps it would be more pragmatic to focus on the environment of what makes the middle school environment so difficult to thrive in.

According to Rockoff and Lockwood (2010), the middle school model is not cost effective over the K-8 model. This suggests that the middle school model needs serious improvement if we are to keep it.

How can we use our knowledge of natural human group sizes to make middle schools more....human? As I discussed earlier, in elementary school, class size matters most. That shouldn't come as a surprise as elementary students spend the majority of each day with the same group of kids and the same teacher in a dedicated classroom. Middle school is where group size gets more complicated.

While class sizes don't differ markedly in the transition to middle school, scheduling schemes do. Elementary students may occasionally have a specialist teacher, but remain with their familiar classroom grouping throughout each day. Middle school students, on the other hand, follow scheduling patterns similar to high school students, with a unique mix of students and a new teacher for typically six class periods per day.

Knowledge of human evolution has illuminated the way for a potentially powerful solution. The academic success of adolescents rests on a return to small-scale hunter-gatherer society. Let's delve deeper into what may be theoretically at work behind what the researchers observed.

Bands and Grade Level Cohorts

Throughout human evolutionary history, we lived and roamed planet earth in smaller groups called bands. A band is the group size that human evolution produced as a solution for the scope of day-to-day life's interactions and support. Bands averaged 42.6 in number (Zhou, 2005), and in our army analogy in the previous section, bands are the platoon.

Multiply the sympathy group (14.3) membership by a factor of roughly 3 and we have a band (Figure 3). Bands are a slightly unstable group that draw membership from a broader pool – from the cognitive group numbering about 150.

Many who have served in a platoon will attest, there is a strength in the connectedness of a group this size. This strength can also be harnessed to enhance learning. This structure doesn't work at the classroom level due to communication bottlenecks and lack of organizational substructure. But if we adjust the grade level cohort to be the size of a band (~45), the structure is provided for a supportive peer group.

Patterning school configuration after the hierarchy of human social group sizes, where cognitive group = school (or functional subdivision), band = grade level cohort, sympathy group = class size, and conversational clique = small group, could provide a powerful solution to the problem of middle school (Figure 3).

Figure 3. Middle School Organization Patterned After the Discrete Hierarchy of Human Social Group Sizes (Left-side of graphic - Data from Zhou, 2005).

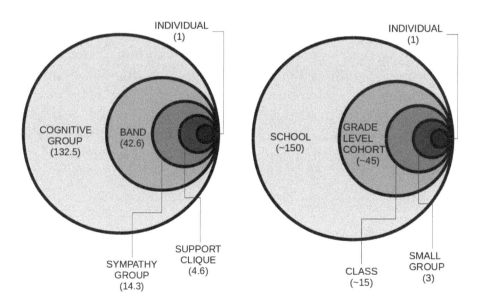

Brain development research suggests middle school is an educationally lucrative time-frame (NIH, 2011) that is too often tragically wasted due to idiosyncrasies between our school culture and human nature. We must have utmost respect for the scale of our humanity during times of special social sensitivity. Our success is predicated on keeping school at a truly human scale. We can't simply warehouse our middle schoolers for three years and lose ground; attention to group sizes is an easy fix.

The middle school years are an inflection point for success or failure later in school. In the middle school studies mentioned above, the data revealed a disturbing downward achievement trajectory from which there was no recovery. Kids at the bottom of the achievement gaps are affected most dramatically. That last statement will start to sound familiar – it's a recurring theme throughout this book. Fixing the conflict with our human biology seems to disproportionately help students at the bottom of the achievement gap. The other side of that coin is that they are disproportionately affected when we get it wrong.

In summary, middle school success depends on a return to small-scale human society. This can change the trajectory of middle school achievement to be a sharply positive one. A safe and cohesive educational environment is essential, and such an environment is only achievable at small scales due to limitations of our brain and our evolutionary psychology. Little Homo Sapiens deserves a grade level cohort size that has been tested by human evolutionary time. Middle school years deserve to be fruitful times of learning, and they can be at school, too!

CHAPTER 5

Small Group Success: Three is a magic number – you hear!

Small groups are regularly used in classrooms. Small groups can allow teachers to group students by varying degrees of skill development or other needs. They also provide the benefit of more active learning, as well as allowing kids to learn from one another.

Small group sizes often range from pairs to small groups of four depending on the nature of the activity, the amount of material resources to share, and limitations to furniture configurations, among other reasons. There are various pros and cons to 2's, 3's, 4's, or more, and we could take up sufficient real-estate brainstorming them all. The focus here is to answer the question: "What is the ideal small group size from the evolutionary point of view"? In this chapter, I will explore small group size in the classroom from the angles of acoustics and human evolution.

Conversational Cliques

The average sized support clique (peoples' inner circle of relationships) is 4.6; these are the people who you would lean on in times of emotional distress or financial ruin (Zhou, 2005) (Table 1, Figure 1). However, this small group is slightly too unwieldy to function efficiently altogether at once in class. Instead, I recommend patterning after a similarly sized social group more fitting for learning environments when a small crew is needed: the conversational clique.

A conversational clique is a human social group consisting of a speaker and active listeners engaged in a conversation. You can observe conversational cliques at parties, in the school commons or cafeteria, and on the playground. Amongst the chitter-chatter of conversational background noise, research shows that the average size of a conversational clique is 3.4, and that additional members drop off quickly in group sizes over 4 (Dunbar, et al, 1995). People simply cannot hear well enough over the background sounds to participate effectively. There is also a natural tendency for people to want to participate equitably in the conversation. That fifth person, and often-times the fourth person to join the conversational clique, is going to wander off to find a new group to chat with. The size of a conversational clique will also decrease as the volume of the background noise increases. This foreshadows trouble in most classrooms.

Technological Limits

Technology has not been able to prevail over this acoustical limitation. Now that we have the ability to virtually connect and video chat with many people thousands of miles apart, it is still difficult to have a conversation with more than four people at a time. When my small family of four tries to communicate with the grandparents on the other end (that makes six) - it is usually a difficult affair. I typically disappear in order to help make the communication easier on the ears. Although it is fabulous to see the in-laws, the same acoustical troubles exist as when we are all in the same room together – even if our actual distance spans from the Pacific to Appalachia. Classroom technology use must be mindful of the conversational clique and human auditory constraints.

Conversational Cliques in the Classroom

Our voices have very real limitations amongst ambient classroom background noise. Imagine a small group of four sitting around a 4-foot diameter (~1.2 meters), circular school activity table. At that distance, four is a somewhat unstable conversational group size amidst the ambient background noise. Large class sizes increase the background noise further. One student in each small group is possibly going to be on the outs, unable to hear partners or be heard effectively amongst the din of the classroom.

As often happens, let's say that the group needs to ask the teacher a question. The teacher comes over – and that makes five! Acoustically speaking, some child from that group has most definitely just been left behind. A group of three allows for a stable conversational group size, and allows for inclusion of an additional voice when necessary (such as the teacher or consultation with an individual from a different group) without losing anyone.

How loud is a classroom – for real?

In 2004-05, someone (McCarty & Rollow) got the idea to examine the background noise level in a typical 4th grade classroom in Los Angeles for two days – when it was occupied with children (Los Angeles Unified School District Acoustical Study in the Student Occupied Classroom).

The researchers first measured background noise in the empty classroom. This could easily be measured during lunch or after school when the room was unoccupied. The American National Standards Institute (ANSI) standard for ambient background noise in an unoccupied classroom is 35 decibels (dB). However, the empty room registered 43-45 dB due to sources such as the HVAC, hums from electronica, and street noise! A silent reading period registered an impressive 45 dB; the kids were either really into their books, or comatose, or some combination thereof. This made the ANSI classroom acoustics standard of 35 dB, determined out of concern for white noise and its potential interference with learning, seem like a lower priority concern.

So it turns out that environmental noise such as ventilation systems, fluorescent humming lights, and traffic on adjacent roads is higher than it should be, but not the biggest source of sound pollution in a classroom. This is obvious to anyone who has been around a group of children. When I ride on a school bus for a field trip, do I ever think to myself, "Hey, the engine on this bus sounds clunky when it accelerates."? No, I do not think that, because I cannot hear myself think, let alone hear the chunking of the motor. Kids are the deafening ambient background noise. Science had triumphantly proven that the kids are the overwhelmingly biggest source of background noise in a classroom. Nobody had ever explored classroom acoustics that deeply before. While not unexpected, the results are nonetheless still shocking. The measurements in the 4th grade class during small group learning activities were between 67-72 dB, and often even louder. That's the volume of a vacuum cleaner; not just the noise from one vacuum from way across the classroom, but vacuum-cleaner-level-noise in everyone's ear-holes throughout the room. According to the sound wave data from the 4th grade classroom, the majority of the time the classroom was occupied with children, the volume was at this high level.

For the majority of the day, in order to be heard or regain the attention of the class during small group work time, the teacher would theoretically need to get the pipes up to 80+ dB when it hits the back row. If it were not impossible, this would be a serious occupational hazard. The other day I met a retired grandmother who was proudly walking her granddaughter to school. The grandmother introduced herself as a former middle school teacher - and that is exactly why she sounded like the gravelly, baritone deejay Shabba Ranks.

Why Can't We Hear the Teacher?

The teacher's voice should be 15 dB greater than the background noise at every point the teacher's voice reaches the students' ears. A teacher's voice should be a certain level higher than the background noise (+15 dB) or else the teacher's words become inaudible. This is called the signal to noise ratio, or the ratio of the teachers voice to the background noise. Adults with typical hearing only need a signal to noise ratio of +6 dB, because their brains have already learned how to fill in missing gaps in language better than kids do – that is why children need the louder +15 dB.

Sound pressure is inversely proportional to the distance from the source. In other words, according to the Inverse Square Law, the teacher's voice fades out quickly as it travels to the back of the classroom and gradually disappears under the ambient noise. Let's walk through a simplified version of what happens as the teacher's voice washes out (please refer to Figure 4: Signal to noise ratio in a typical classroom).

Figure 4. Signal to noise ratio in a typical classroom.
The teacher's voice (which should be +15 dB when it reaches each student) is quickly extinguished due to the inverse square law and ambient background noise.

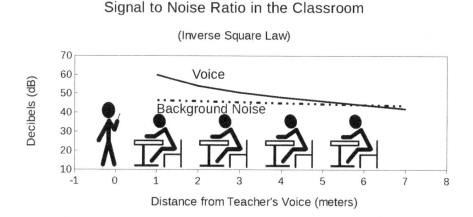

In a typical 'quiet' classroom, when all kids are sitting still and lips are zipped, we can measure a teacher's loud and clear voice at about 60 dB from a distance of one meter in front of her face. The background noise is about 45 dB. For every doubling of distance, the teacher's voice loses 6 dB of steam, or drops by 50%, as the sound pressure waves radiate outward across an increasingly greater area. (Please refer to Figure 4 above.) A kid who is sitting in the front row - about 1 meter from the teacher, completely in the blast zone, who can smell the coffee that the teacher drank for breakfast, is hearing the teacher at 15 dB above background. Everything is great except the coffee breath. The kid seated 2 meters away from the teacher is only hearing the instruction at 9 dB above background. At 5 meters away (16.4 feet), the ratio between the teacher and the background noise is one and the same. The students in the back rows are just as likely to learn a math lesson from the HVAC as they are from the teacher.

Our fears are fact: the classroom is a lousy acoustical environment. The average classroom acoustical environment is so poor that a rational person would think that speaking, the primary and preferred method of learning used in classrooms, would not be a viable strategy. It is the paradox of the primary way humans communicate rendering their environment unfit for using such communication. The implications for students who are learning English, who have hearing problems, who have sensory processing difficulties, or who have the bad luck of sitting in the back row, are of even greater significance.

Noise Pollution Solution

Because social, small group learning is a learning orientation that kids generally prefer, and because it is theoretically a useful strategy, it is essential that effective communication be acoustically possible in the first place. Unfortunately, even in 1st grade, the 'solution' is often silence, and silence is exalted as a characteristic of being a good student.

One solution to this acoustical problem is to set small group sizes to 3 students. Setting these groups at 3 helps to make this learning configuration acoustically feasible in typical (typically loud, that is) classrooms. Ultimately, no matter how much acoustical engineering we try to throw at the classroom, the volume in the classroom has a great deal to do with the number of people in the room – and without addressing class size and the volume produced by the masses, we will continue to be dumbfounded by the mystery of what should be an effective learning strategy rendered useless.

Special Considerations

Although sound pressure levels can be measured, there is variation in how the brain perceives loudness amongst different people, and how it reacts as well. For students with sensory processing disorder (SPD), which often can be found in students with Autism Spectrum Disorder (ASD) and Attention Deficit Hyperactivity Disorder (ADHD), sound levels tolerable to others can be quite stressful or even unbearable. Unfortunately, this may add enough stress to shut down the learning process. The vacuum cleaner volume typical in classrooms during small group learning activities can be a hostile environment for a significant portion of the special needs population as well as for more typical students. Again, small group size in the context of appropriate class size is key.

Gender: Cutting through the static

Another acoustical dilemma emerges in the later half of the middle school years: The downward pitch-shift of the teenage male voice is coupled with an increase in overall body size. This not only allows for increased vocal volume, but also a booming frequency that can more easily cut through the background racket. A study (Dunbar, et al, 1997) showed that when a male and female are paired together, the time conversing is shared equally, 50/50. However, as the group size expands, the percentage of time a female group member participates equitably diminishes. One explanation has to do with the frequency of the female voice. This higher pitched frequency cannot be heard as well as the lower pitched male voice in a loud environment. Other evolutionary explanations consider the possibility of females assessing 'advertising' by male voices, rather than speaking themselves. Regardless, smaller small-group sizes may create a more equitable situation.

There has been much speculation about how classroom discussions can be dominated by male voices. This tendency is especially concerning in subject areas where a negative stereotype about female performance exists. An evolutionary explanation gives a fresh take on the situation. Nevertheless, this perspective raises some alarms about group dynamics, and how the auditory landscape may cause trouble for female students. Hopefully being armed with this information can help educators to more readily identify solutions for small group success.

Benefits of the Small Group

Before leaving the small group topic, let's get to the heart of the true benefits of the small group. Why do we choose to arrange in small groups in the first place – aside from providing a smaller radius from which to distribute glue sticks? Small groups are where coordination is simpler and communication can flow more freely and equitably. The real advantage of the small group may not be in simply adding a diversity of skills, but also a diversity of thoughts and perspectives.

Humans are great at copying. The great thing about

learning with friends is that they are going to "filter" (Rendell, 2010) information for you. A friend is not going to show you their worst dance move, or not even their mediocre dance moves, they are only going to share their best dance moves with you - only the best for you. Not only will they share the good stuff, they may know your thinking well enough to explain it in a way that you understand.

When learning, information is inadvertently filtered by fellow students, which helps to aid in comprehension by allowing students to hear an alternate, perhaps more relevant or eloquent, explanation. Inadvertent filtering can take place when another student explains a concept from their point of view. Filtering is just as natural as a mommy bird chewing up the worm for the baby bird. It makes it a whole lot easier to digest. Studying by yourself does not afford this same opportunity for academic worm regurgitation. Filtering is a powerful academic benefit performed by nature. Sometimes, the teacher or text just doesn't have the right approach to make it click for every student straight-away.

When students combine filtering with the interpersonal knowledge that is possible in smaller group sizes, learning can be much easier. Small group sessions add benefits to learning because of a phenomenon called Theory of Mind. The ability of other students to 'think about what others are thinking' enhances the dynamism and productivity of the group, and makes filtering even more efficacious.

There are many factors that play into determining a small group size. If we set our small group sizes up in a way that leverages our biology, rather than works at odds with it – only then can we really harness the power of small group learning. When this can be done in concert with biologically-appropriate sized classes and schools, we will be primed for the real educational reform that is needed. From an evolutionary point of view on schools, three is a magic number!

PART II

In the Beginning was the Word

CHAPTER 6

Dialect Division: The hidden trouble with racial categorization for tracking achievement gaps in an increasingly diverse America

Imagine if the late and infamously erratic Libyan leader Muammar Qaddafi traveled through time to become a new student at a public school in the United States today. This might sound like a more ominous version of the movie *Coming to America* (1998), but hang in there. If dressed anything like his speech at the United Nations in 2009, many Americans would perceive Muammar to be straight out of a circa-1990 Afrocentric Hip Hop video. Now, envision a teen Qaddafi with an Afro-esque hairstyle standing there dressed in the manner of the pan-African phase of his tenure, with a traditional black, woolen checheya hat on his head and an over-sized Africa pendant on his chest. He waits patiently while his mom fills out the registration paperwork, and marks the 'white' racial category box in accordance with the directions.

Later on, during his first day at high school, Muammar ends up eating lunch with some kids who can speak Arabic, and who used to be part of the district's English Language Learner program. They explain to him how to not dress like an immigrant, and yet are intrigued by the boldness of his fashion. That's right, the Arabic-speaking immigrant from Africa is categorized simply as "white" in our public school system. This is the reality of the strange, arbitrary, and invented world of racial categories used by public schools. As you can imagine, these categories also lead to equally confusing interpretations of academic achievement.

Race is one of the primary pieces of demographic information a school collects about its students. However, this practice may run counter to human evolution. Our hunter-gatherer ancestors would have had to travel a long way down the genetic gradient highway in order to interact with enough people of markedly different skin tones to come up with a color-coded classification system. More importantly, this racial category information may fail to provide the information needed to identify achievement gaps.

As a social species that evolved to strategically make use of coalitions, cues to whose side of the fence you are on are a crucial piece of information. For evolutionary reasons, people automatically register the life-stage and gender of people that they meet. Experimentally though, race has been elusive as an obligatory piece of social information that humans collect on each other. The importance of race diminishes in circumstances where stronger clues to alliance are present (Kurzban, 2001) (Voorspoels, et al, 2014). A sports team affiliated color-scheme can provide just such a clue.

I will share a common story of allegiances. On a rainy fall Sunday in the Pacific Northwest, I went to the market on Seahawk Sunday, obliviously dressed in the black and yellow of the opposing rival Pittsburgh Steelers football team. Even the cashiers were contractually dressed in green, blue, and gray. The strong and unanimous looks of condemnation from across the ethnic spectrum were understandable once I realized the circumstances. In the social and historical reality many people live under, skin color has simply become a cheat-sheet for coalition – a team uniform for when there isn't a team uniform.

I will use the question posed by the title of Beverly Daniel Tatum's (1997) text *'Why are all the Black Kids Sitting Together in the Cafeteria?'* to dig deeper into racial categories, how coalitions are aligned, who is sitting next to who, and how it relates to achievement gaps.

Race & Ethnicity Categories at School

My son's school enrollment paperwork required a 'race and

ethnicity' form to be filled out. First off on the form, you are either Latino or not Latino. Check that. Next on the list comes white. There was no white subcategory of Leprechaun available, but at least I considered trying to warn them.

Next on the survey comes black, if you are black, you're black. Again, just like white, there is just one lonely category. As I described in the Qaddafi example, the white category includes African ethnic groups from north of the Sahara. The 'black' category, which contains most of the planet's human genetic and cultural diversity, is the strangest place to find an umbrella catch-all category. Even though the public school Home Language Survey is published in three different Ethiopian languages in my state, (Amharic, Oromo, Tigrinya), if you have had any sub-Saharans in your lineage, this sole black category is for you.

Asians get to pick from 16 popular flavors such as Japanese and Vietnamese. Sailing east out onto the Liquid Continent, there are 9 different categorical choices from across the Pacific: Melanesian, Micronesian, Samoan... Then comes the choice explosion: Washington State is comprised of a large number of indigenous tribal entities, many of which are independent, sovereign governments, and so there are over 30 in a long list of Washington's Native American Tribes to choose from. There is also the ability to check multiple categories if your race and ethnicity necessitates, or check other.

Some of the most diverse schools in America are found south of Seattle, Washington. The Tukwila School District was ranked by the *New York Times* in 2009 to be the most diverse district in the USA. A few miles further down Interstate 5, the Federal Way School District lists 105 different foreign languages spoken at home as recorded on its Home Language Survey. These are among the most diverse schools in the United States, and hot-spots of linguistic and cultural diversity. So my question is, in an increasingly multi-ethnic America, how relevant is race in statistically tracking achievement gaps between categorical groups, where the groups may be composed of somewhat ambiguous and arbitrary populations?

For now, I want to put aside the race and ethnicity categories as a basis for tracking achievement gaps. There is other data that is already currently collected by most districts which may give a crisper picture of academic achievement between subgroups.

Language & How Humans Associate

For as long as modern humans have been around, we have separated ourselves by dialect. Dialects form very readily in human language – some say almost spontaneously. Throughout human evolutionary history, dialects have been the primary way to determine who is in our group and who is not. Dialects are mostly innate, imprinted early in childhood and we consider those who share our native dialects to be inherently more honest, trustworthy, and friendly. Scientists think that this provided a reliable means of controlling the problem of free riders in society – those who take advantage of others (Dunbar, 1996). Dialects can be found according to socio-economic status, generation, gender, ethnicity, geography, profession, and many other social divisions.

In a clever dialect experiment (Kinzler, 2009), young kindergarten-aged children were asked to choose who they would want to become friends with. They chose kids who spoke their native tongue over kids who spoke foreign languages or had foreign accents. This was true even if the kids had different skin pigmentation. The children could understand the speakers with foreign accents, but they recognized them as being different, and chose to be friends with kids who spoke the same way as them. Only when the children were silent did they pick kids that matched their skin color to be friends with. Otherwise, skin color lost out to dialect when children were choosing friends. Children separate themselves into groups the same way our ancient hunter-gatherer ancestors would have.

The human geography of the cafeteria or anywhere else can largely be predicted by dialect. Maybe a group of black kids in the cafeteria are sitting together because they are all speaking the same dialect. But, maybe this is a more diverse school. Maybe 'all' of the 'black' kids aren't sitting near each other. Maybe some are, but if we take a closer look, we may see something else. We may see a group of three Wolof speakers sitting way over there, and a table of half a dozen bilingual Amharic speakers at another table. Several tables of kids that may appear to be homogeneously white may actually be broken down into tables of dialect differences varied by economic class. A few white Russian or Ukrainian immigrants form their own conversational cliques, separate from white kids who speak English as a first language. Perhaps there is an immigrant table of multilingual loose-ends, not finding a critical mass large enough to speak their native tongue with, so they converse in the common denominator – the same level of ESL (English as a Second Language). A few kids may even be talking together in the language of a particular shared interest – like soccer. But what does all of this lunchroom talk among friends have to do with tracking achievement gaps?

Dialect & Achievement Gaps

Just when you thought race was the most intractable issue in American education, now we have a new achievement gap that comes to the surface. If dialect is powerful enough to determine who little kids want to be friends with, it surely plays a more important role at school than we have ever given it credit for.

In 2011, the Seattle Public School District was surprised when they discovered a discrepancy between sub-groups of black students on Washington's state standardized test (*Seattle Times*, 2011) (Figure 5). In math, kids who spoke Amharic at home, a language native to Ethiopia, scored 62%; black kids who spoke English at home were significantly lower at 36%. Seventy percent was the district average in math for all kids. In reading, Amharic speakers scored 74%, while the black kids who spoke English at home scored 56%; the district average was 78%. The data did not include those enrolled in English Language Learner (ELL) programs, who typically have lower test scores.

While both populations were classified in the black racial category on school enrollment paperwork, there was a major difference between the two groups' performance levels. A 26% spread in math and an 18% difference in reading are large achievement gaps between these black student sub-populations. The use of racial category greatly obscures the true academic attainment of both sub-populations. If we are using our data to recognize areas for improvement, we should be smart about it. Perhaps we should be using a demographic with greater relevance than race in an increasingly diverse America. If we are not sitting at the same cafeteria table together, we might not be doing our homework together either.

Figure 5. Achievement Gap Between 'Black' Students in Seattle Schools by Home Language (*Seattle Times*, 2011). *Students enrolled in English Language Learner Programs not included

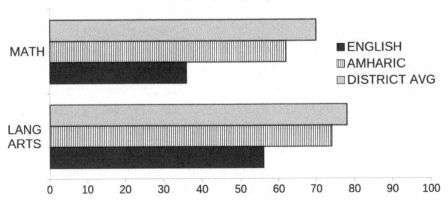

Why Track Education Statistics by Race

So why do schools track racial groups? The US Department of Education is clear that racial and ethnicity tracking is meant to track socio-economic factors, not biological or genetic factors which racial groups do not represent. At this point, we've made a case that: 1) Schools track achievement by the demographic category of race, which consists of somewhat arbitrary groupings. 2) Kids have a natural tendency to group themselves by dialect. 3) Differences in achievement gaps may be seen when students are grouped according to home language. Examining achievement gaps by home language may be the more appropriate demographic to use in identifying achievement gaps. Home language, when used either alone or in conjunction with race, may bring greater intention to the Department of Education's socio-economic purpose for tracking school data by racial categories.

What Achievement Gaps Tell Us

Now that we have discussed alternative ways of identifying sub-populations suffering from achievement gaps, we would be remiss in not interpreting why we have racial and economic achievement gaps in the first place. No matter how we go about grouping the student population, we still have a problem with some groups doing significantly better than others. I will now demonstrate that: 1) Genes have the biggest impact on academic performance. 2) These genes conferring academic achievement are distributed similarly in all populations of people, regardless of race or class. 3) In the US, kids from low-income households are prevented from using their innate intelligence to succeed.

Academic Achievement and Genetics

In 2013 there was a large and robust UK study (sample size

of over 11,000) of 16 year-olds' academic abilities that controlled for both environment and genetics. It accomplished this by studying the academic achievement of identical (genetically identical) and fraternal twins (50% of genes in common) (Shakeshaft, et al, 2013). This study demonstrated that genetics explained the largest variation in academic performance on the GSCE (General Certificate of Secondary Education). This study was able to provide strong evidence due to its massive sample size. The "strong genetic influence" on test scores meant that almost 60% of the overall test score was attributed to heredity. A shared environment accounted for 36% of the score.

Of that 36% of GSCE test score variance determined by shared environment, 10%-15% is attributable to neighborhood. A shared home environment and parenting accounted for another chunk of 20-25%. There is a dwindling range of percentage points that can be attributed to school or individual teacher effectiveness. Unless... you live in the United States.

Poverty and Intelligence Genes at US Schools

This 60% contribution of genetics to academic achievement that I mentioned earlier is true for Australia, the UK, and other European countries. However, in the US, a meager 24% of genetics contribute to academic achievement of low socio-economic (low-SES) kids (Tucker-Drob & Bates, 2015). What this means is that in the US school system, kids from low-income backgrounds can only make limited use of their own natural-born intelligence that they already possess to advance their academic abilities. The American Dream doesn't seem to play out as promised. Hence, academic achievement gaps between these kids and their more affluent peers persist.

The authors of this research (Tucker-Drob & Bates, 2015) propose that these differences may be due to the fact that social and health disparities are better dealt with in western countries outside the US. While these disparities undoubtedly play a role, there is more to this story.

I speculate that schools are a large contributor to this under-achievement. The school system blindly imposes unnecessary obstacles so that students cannot capitalize on their own natural-born intellect. This text will continue to identify and provide practical remedies to these barriers. Students living in poverty typically face differential discipline, larger class sizes, psychological threats, lower-quality instructional methods, lower physical activity levels, less recess time, and even less time to eat lunch (Cohen, 2016) at school. These barriers are not without biological consequences to academic achievement.

Schools should not be in the business of thwarting kids' inherent intelligence. When Little Homo Sapiens faces so many obstacles to employing his natural human super-powers at school, his performance pays the price.

Because the genes underlying intelligence and academic achievement are found in every population, the bell curves of test score distributions for every demographic group should all line up and superimpose right on top of each other. We would see the same range of achievement for every population. But our schools do not show such outcomes.

With the knowledge that race or class is not synonymous with genetics or the genes for academic achievement, a sad truth about our education system comes to light. The more influence that genes have on test scores, the more achievement gaps can be viewed as a direct measure of inequality in the system (Shakeshaft, 2013). These achievement gaps can be viewed as a school inequality index: a cumulative measure of the educational system's affronts to the evolutionary human biology of students.

While schools often point to race, poverty, social, and cultural factors beyond their control to explain achievement gaps, it is time for schools to take greater responsibility. I argue that addressing that responsibility means examining the differential impacts of school on the evolutionary biology of students lagging in achievement. Correctly identifying and characterizing achievement gaps through this evolutionary lens is essential.

In Summary

- Humans naturally segregate themselves by dialect. It may be appropriate to use dialect to identify achievement gaps between sub-groups rather than racial categories.

- Genetics underlying intelligence do not differ by racial category or economic class, though academic progress does differ on average by racial category and socio-economic status. Schools can use disparate scores as an index of inequality between populations that schools must take some responsibility for.

- Exam scores are largely a reflection of genetics favoring academic achievement. This is not true for students of low socio-economic status, whose own genetic propensity to learn is cut by more than half.

- Students living in poverty in the United States are dramatically stymied in benefiting from their own intelligence. These barriers should be identified and engineered out of the system. This is indeed the mission of this text.

CHAPTER 7

200 Minutes of Vitamin G: Capitalizing on gossip, the most essential language art

Envision the commonplace scene of a teacher giving instructions. The teacher is interrupted (and students are distracted) by a pair of chatty kids. The teacher politely redirects the students' attentions, regains the attention of the class, and continues. Thirty seconds later, the teacher is distracted again by the same pair who now must stand by the teacher, which temporarily kills the banter. Another group in the back starts to exchange quips and giggle, and the teacher drops their names sternly to cease the dialogue and demand their attention. The process is repeated until a version of Whack-A-Mole ensues with student conversations uprising seemingly spontaneously. The teacher is now using a loud voice to stay above the fray of collective chit-chat and forces through quickly to the end of the instruction.

What you have just witnessed is a futile struggle against nature, a conflict that comprises a large portion of each and every school day. Some teachers may feel it reflects poorly on their classroom management abilities. Many classroom management strategies are based around creating barriers to gossip: seating charts separating loquacious friends, proximity of the teacher to chatty kids, tricks to re-gain attention like bells or clapping, giving five, etc. It may relieve teachers to know that the ability to gossip is the result of many thousands of years of evolution – it is a defining characteristic of our species. When it is put that way, classroom management struggles and realities come into the light.

Using fMRI to image the brain, a study revealed that it is intrinsically rewarding for people to talk about themselves (Tamir and Mitchell, 2012). About 30-40% of what comes out of your mouth is talking about yourself. Talking about yourself is not only a universal need, but it makes us feel good, too. The collective biological drive for students to start talking about themselves, all of the time, can be overwhelming. Educators must seek a deep understanding of this fundamental aspect of our social biology. It is only then that the teacher can master how to flow with nature, artfully flipping a chronic disturbance into an asset.

As mentioned earlier in our small group analysis, students prefer to learn in small groups through talking. The opportunity for casual social conversation surely plays into this preference. What else would you expect from a juvenile of an obligate social species? A leopard cannot change its spots any more than a human can function without verbal social interaction, so the classroom proceedings must adapt.

The word gossip carries a somewhat negative connotation with it (Dunbar, 2004). The standard dictionary definition of gossip embodies the 'talking shit behind someone's back' aspect of the term. The Oxford Dictionary (US English Edition) defines gossip:

> "Casual or unconstrained conversation or reports about other people, typically involving details that are not confirmed as being true."

Scientists theorize that sharing negative information about somebody is another way that humans control the problem of free-riders in society: those that take advantage without giving back. And while that is an important evolutionary function, it only comprises 5% of our social conversation. For the other 95%, we are mostly exchanging social information (Dunbar, et al, 1997) and other benign topics such as upcoming events or clothes. It's time to re-imagine gossip in a broader sense. So just relax your mind as we zoom out to view the bigger picture – let's give gossip a fresh start, free from its slanderous baggage.

In this chapter, I will flip the script and explore why schools need to come to grips with gossip: its universality, its function, why it is necessary, and its time demands. Ultimately, I will explain why we need to understand that gossip is indeed, without exaggeration, the pinnacle of human evolution, and how we can turn this perceived disruption into an educational asset.

Bonding

Imagine a pair of chimps lounging around, taking turns combing through and picking bugs and debris out of each other's hair. Chimp bonding sounds a little bit creepy to me, but it is a friendly enough vision to have. Primates such as chimps leverage their relationships by physically grooming one another – mutual flea plucking. This is a one-on-one activity that is a time-consuming yet essential bonding ritual. It pays off when the individual is in need of support or must rally backup for protection. The arboreal ancestors of humans did the same.

Nevertheless, there is more to life than grooming. As our ancestor's came down from the trees and moved out onto open land, their social networks had to increase in size to ensure safety. Our ancestors would have come up against a grooming time-crunch in order to have enough hours left over to acquire food, sleep, and do everything else they needed to do.

Proponents of Social Brain Theory (Dunbar, 1998) hypothesize that our large brains evolved the capacity for speech and language to solve this grooming time-crunch – to bond through gossip rather than grooming. With the capacity of speech and language, the human brain could now replace physical grooming with verbal grooming. Social conversation became the new version of manual grooming. Not only can we talk with multiple partners at once (up to three other people at a time), but we can keep track of friends and relatives who aren't even present.

For example, when I see my Mom, I inquire about my brothers, aunts and uncles, cousins, etc. I can get up to speed on the whole clan when I may only personally see them once a year. Additionally, humans can walk and talk at the same time, despite being generally lousy multi-taskers. We can make social conversation while eating, running, foraging, farming, preparing food, caring for children, and so on. Gossip is a superb substitute for physical grooming, enough to drive the evolution of the human brain's neocortex to leverage around 150 people.

A common complaint about students is that they socialize too much. Imagine how many parent-teacher conferences at school include this nagging issue. A student's chatter is distracting to others. A student's talk is disruptive to the teacher's instruction. Off-topic talking takes up too much class time, interfering with the class's ability to learn. How can something that just feels so natural, be so wrong in the school environment?

It is important to pause and consider the irony: The chatty student is doing exactly what they evolved to do, and apparently, to the dismay of the teacher, doing it better than everybody else. In an evolutionary sense, this is the hallmark of a successful human being. This social propensity will probably serve this student well throughout their lifetime – most likely, more than the academic topic at hand will. As teachers, it's easy to project that the ultimate purpose of the brain must be to crunch calculus problems or write essays. The inherent capabilities of the human brain to handle these relatively new cultural innovations should not detract from the brain's much older social function. The things that have given humans an evolutionary advantage throughout the age of *Homo sapiens* will most likely continue to do so. It is time to start viewing our strengths as our strengths, starting priority-wise with the traits that make us successful humans in the first place.

Sacrifices

To solve this socializing-as-disruption problem, teachers

must be prepared to make a sacrifice to our humanity. Rather, we must be prepared to 'give up' a certain amount of time in order to quell a quintessentially human need to gossip. So what is the cost? How large is the sacrifice? Anthropological research across cultures shows that 20% of our waking hours are spent in social conversation (Dunbar, 1996). This comes out to roughly 3 hours and 15 minutes of each day. This is the price of our species' success, the cost to maintain our web of relationships with ~150 individuals. And while it may consume a fifth of each day, gossip takes a whole lot longer to accomplish when the teacher keeps interrupting!

Schools can't ignore that we are a species that must spend one out of five waking minutes in social conversation. It is time to turn to nature-patterning to implement a more harmonious classroom experience. If we picture this 20% rule at school, it translates to 12 minutes of every hour-long class period, or 1 out of every 5 days over the course of a week. Now that we know the cost, how can a teacher manage and capitalize on this phenomenon?

Remember, humans can verbally socialize while multitasking. We may not be able to send text-messages and drive, but we can talk and perform other easily-automated physical tasks. Is there a 12-minute block of class time where students are doing something routine and may be free to converse while accomplishing the task? This is where the art of teaching comes in: effectively integrating the opportunity for social exchanges in order to help students obtain the recommended daily allowance of vitamin G (roughly 200 minutes of gossip per day). How does the arrangement of the classroom help to facilitate easy social exchange? How does the design of the overall school schedule work to accommodate this need? How do classroom learning experiences make room for this provision? How does the arrangement of informal spaces on the school campus work to promote small group conversation? A more sophisticated approach in the classroom may be for teachers to intentionally incorporate gossip into the lesson, allowing for an exchange of social information that parallels the topic of study.

Conclusion

It will require a paradigm shift to think of social conversation as something other than a waste of instructional hours. However, these gossip hours are an investment, especially if orchestrated with pro-social outcomes in mind. Humans use gossip to maintain social cohesion. A capital investment in the social cohesion of the class may yield a more productive learning environment. Greater interpersonal knowledge of classmates can surely add greater insight into how students explain concepts to one another and operate as a team. A better connected, and as a result, safer and more trusting social learning environment will likely have better academic outcomes than a stifled class that can't stop thinking that they would rather be conversing with their friends.

Gossip time as an essential and universal human need requires closer examination of how and when this need is accomplished, and amongst what sized groups at school. The consequence of running afoul of this human need is evident in the daily discipline struggles of classrooms. A fight this futile must come to an end. What if social conversation for 20% of the day became a school rule, rather than a chronically violated school rule. After all, it is one of the core, unwritten rules of our species. The success of the social learning environment, and our students' success as individuals at school also depends on it. When we incorporate gossip time into schools that are patterned after natural social group sizes, we lay the foundation for a connected social climate that encourages learning.

PART III
Ecology

CHAPTER 8

Must Get High in Class: Classroom management based on the Brain Opioid Theory of Social Attachment

Around 450 million years ago, back when your great-great-...great-... grandmother was around, looking like a fish that evolved jaws for the first time, there was already something special about her DNA that you would one day inherit. Molecular evidence tells us that she already had the genes for all four types of opiate receptors that humans have today (Dreborg, et al, 2008). And as I will explain, knowledge of the endogenous opiate system gives us the power to interpret the classroom like a magic crystal ball – only it's just science.

Endogenous Opiates

Endogenous opiates are chemicals produced by your own body that provide natural pain relief and tolerance, as well as euphoric feelings. They are produced in response to pain and stress and serve as an important survival mechanism. The pain of going hungry drives us to find food which in-turn tastes amazing when we eat it. Sunshine on your shoulders makes you happy as it provides warmth and promotes vitamin D production. The pain of social isolation and relationship heartbreak reinforces the need for social behavior. The reward and pain tolerance from long hours of manual labor or a runner's high keeps us going when the going gets tough.

You have likely experienced the effects of these endogenous opiates after a hard day's work, after enjoying an evening of laughter with friends and family, or from singing along with your favorite song. These endogenous opiates cause a strong physical dependency, and a deficiency in these endogenous opiates also serves as punishment. This endogenous opioid system has been driving animal behavior for survival for nearly half of a billion years. This alone warrants greater attention to how this biochemistry influences behavior in the classroom.

The opiate drugs like heroin, morphine, and oxycodone bind to the same μ (mu) opioid receptor that our bodies' own endogenously-produced opioids do. It is no wonder these drugs are so highly addictive and end up quickly hijacking an addict's behavior for the purpose of drug acquisition. However, this ancient and primitive pain/reward aspect of our endogenous opioid system is only the beginning of this system's story.

Positive Social Reinforcement

Chimpanzees are our primate relatives, and just as our common ancestor did, they use physical grooming as a bonding mechanism: a way of maintaining social ties and strategically reinforcing alliances. Tugging of hair during grooming is mildly painful - enough to cause a release of endogenous opiates. Getting high off of hair-pulling is set deep in our social primate evolutionary history. The opiates produced during this grooming ritual may have become re-purposed to serve an additional role in maintaining our social bonds. The evolution of this additional function for endogenous opiates is named BOTSA, or the Brain Opioid Theory of Social Attachment (Machin & Dunbar, 2011). That's right, not only do these opiates help with pain tolerance and survival, but they also help us maintain our network of family and friends.

A definitive characteristic of humans and other primates is our unique social biology. It makes sense that a 'social compass' of sorts evolved in humans to be integrated into our behavioral survival mechanism. Social behavior is so integral for human survival that it is hard-wired into our endogenous opiate pain/reward system. Endogenous opiates keep us coming back for more positive social interactions. Americans can see the devastating consequences of this biological 'social compass' being overridden in opiate addicts. Even the closest relationships are destroyed when a naturally balanced mechanism promoting positive social behavior is wrecked. Because we owe our success as a species to our social brains, we must take these naturally produced opiates, and the social context they are produced in, and evolved in, very seriously.

Less Hair Pulling, More Talking, & A Problem

Enter the naked ape – *Homo sapiens*. We style each others hair, but the amount of time we spend is miniscule compared with the hours logged by other great apes in grooming. As we discussed in the previous section, our primate ancestors used physical grooming to produce endogenous opiates in order to bond, just like our chimp cousins do. Humans likely need these endogenous opiates to bond as well – but need another way for our bodies to produce them, as we replaced manual grooming with gossip.

Touch releases endogenous opiates – when a mom gives her child a hug, for example. Exchanging a relaxing shoulder massage or when partners have sexual relations are other examples of physical, endogenous opiate releasing activities amongst humans. But these types of exchanges are obviously not for school.

So how do humans make up for this shortfall in opiate-producing physical grooming activities? We don't, not in these modern times anyway. This is partially why the line at the pharmacy is bigger than it should be and epidemic levels of addiction are gripping the neighborhood, nation, and world. Aside from human touch, there are only a few behaviors which can stimulate a release of endogenous opiates. These activities are considered "pro-social" because they produce the biochemical glue (opiates) in our brains that hold our relationships together. Pay attention if you are a teacher reading this; this next box will become our new central dogma of classroom management:

> **Performing the following non-touch social activities releases endogenous opiates:**
>
> (1) vigorous movement (such as running, dancing)
> (2) laughter
> (3) music
>
> Doing these activities synchronously in groups significantly magnifies the response! (Cohen, *et al,* 2010) (Dunbar, 2011)

Hacking Student Behavior: A case study

I came across a story about Gildo Rey Elementary (Auburn School District, northeast of Tacoma, WA), which was showcased in the *Seattle Times* as a part of its *Education Lab* series. Despite having a high poverty rate (as measured by 88% free or reduced price meals), nearly 95% of 4th graders at Gildo Rey passed that state's math assessment in 2013. That level of achievement would bring envy from most any public school, regardless of its demographics. Somewhat controversially, the teachers achieved the result with a method referred to as direct instruction, or what *Seattle Times* education reporter Linda Shaw described as

> "a fast-paced call-and-response approach that critics deride as 'kill and drill'."

While the class sizes at this school weren't overly large, they were clearly above the top range for the sympathy group. This may have driven the instructional style of the teachers towards direct instruction as the viable option. Direct instruction is where the teacher has control of the invisible microphone, directs the information flow, and expects students to respond with an expected answer. Regardless of the reason for the method, this is the method chosen by the instructors and success depends on making that direct instruction method work to the best of its ability. Those kind of scores, which climbed steadily over the years, were the result of consistent, repetitive, engaging, quick-paced instruction, with a lot of time on task, along with coordinated efforts by the staff. At least that is how the explanation went.

But there is something else at play here. I would like to provide an alternate interpretation of the success of this school using the Brain Opioid Theory of Social Attachment. In short, the teachers turned math lessons into something mildly rhythmic and musical. These teachers owe their success to utilizing a pedagogical 'hack' to juvenile human neurobiology.

In search for the truth, I feel like I have officially reached the awkward point in this nature documentary narration: To prevent loud socializing or distracting movement from busting out, and to prevent kids giving up on a tough problem too easily, the teacher needs to keep the kids high on drugs. However, the drugs I am referring to are simply the ones manufactured naturally by the students' own bodies. The teacher is leading a group music session – and thus, tapping into the students endogenous opiate system. I know its weird to think about it that way, but it is a much needed perspective. Students may yield their need to socialize or behave distractingly for these endogenous opiates to some degree, – and that is power.

Now, in using a direct instructional style, the teacher is on a path where they need to be "on" all of the time. They must continually work at keeping the endogenous opioids flowing in the students' brains. In the *Seattle Times* interview, this can be seen when the teacher is talking about the instructional style at the school, and had this to say:

"...and they respond to that, and it is hard, but it, its just a, its a craft – and you have to work at it."

That craft is honing a positive feedback loop of endogenous opiate highs and academic success. Let's take a closer look.

Music in a Group Setting

Music, in this case, the teacher's vocal inflections and staccato statements, provides a predictable rhythm for the students to answer the teacher's call-and-response queries in unison. The students participate in communal music making with their responses. The synchronization, exertion, and music are all known to stimulate endogenous opiate release, especially in group settings.

Endogenous opiates help mediate social bonding and promote positive social feelings. Working together in a groove promotes endogenous opiate releases; the positive feelings and pro-social atmosphere in-turn promote more of this behavior. In this case, the behavior involved repetition of math concepts and related problem solving. This is reflected in the comments by a girl who had struggled with the process of division before coming to the school. She said at the end of the interview that math was her favorite class because it was "easy, and fun."

As the person in control of the classroom, and leading the call-and-response, the teacher is in the position of drug dealer. In order to keep control of the floor verbally, and maintain effectiveness, the teacher needs to maintain the musicality, thus maintaining timely drug delivery before the students go looking somewhere else for the stuff (chatting, laughing, moving, etc.). Boosting the social-bonding endogenous opiates in the brains of students will help give them the positive affect, resilience, and tolerance of struggle they need to stick with learning math from day-to-day.

While this rhythm-infused instructional style may not be new anthropologically, it may be a cultural change for many

United States classrooms. Take the following quote from Permaculture pioneer Bill Mollison, who uses nature-patterning for building sustainable agricultural systems:

> "You have a cultural method of work and a cultural method of learning. In Africa, everybody sings. They sing the work, they sing the learning, they sing the story from village to village. To me, the sound of people singing while they work is Africa. We won't find that in Europe"
>
> – Bill Mollison (1991) *Global Gardener with Bill Mollison. (Part I: The Tropics)*. Bullfrog Films: DVD ISBN: 1-59458-423-0

The importance of music and synchrony while working allows us to predict the movements of others more reliably. You can avoid accidents this way and work more efficiently. While enduring hard manual labor, singing helps to raise endogenous opiate levels, which result in higher pain tolerance. The release of neurochemicals that result in euphoric feelings may encourage the hard work to proceed. The positive feedback loop of pro-social behavior amongst peers along with endogenous opiate reward, all-the-while encoding the message in the music for memory, seems like a whiz-bang strategy.

These methods are increasingly used by charter schools, where instruction in an algebra class may include rote call-and-response of math formulas. A synchronized hand clap may follow after a student attempts an answer to a problem. It may sound like a nerd army jogging in formation during a basic training exercise in front of a white-board, but it can deliver positive results. Musical, synchronous behavior keeps the dope flowing and keeps kids more socially at ease, while increasing their pain tolerance to struggle positively towards learning goals. With this new found rhythm at school, all of a sudden the skills required for teaching start to look more like the skills of a Hip Hop Emcee than those of a teacher.

Group Laughter

No child should go a day at school without laughing hard with their friends, and for a good reason. Endogenous opiates are released in response to laughter (Dunbar, 2011), especially in a social group setting. Pain tolerance is used to indirectly measure endogenous opiate levels. In one such experiment, a group of test subjects watched *Episode 95 of South Park (My Future Self N' Me)*, while researchers humanely pumped up a pressure cuff around their arms until they tapped out. The episode's 'drug use prevention' theme was mirrored by a factual drug documentary viewed by a control group. Laughter boosted the subjects opiate levels and thus, their tolerance to pain (Dunbar, 2011). So there you have it, laughter makes people feel nice!

Theoretically, humor can also be used to maintain student attention and boost achievement in the same way that music and vigorous activity can; however, this requires the aforementioned humor to be humorous enough to generate spontaneous laughter from all students, again and again. The learning should ideally be encoded in the humor. If you have ever heard a classroom having a good time from a distance down the hall, you can hear that the laughter of the children is also highly synchronous. The laughter flares up and tapers off roughly altogether. Relaxed social laughter like this is an excellent group bonding mechanism and provides the pain tolerance to stick it out through tough challenges.

What often makes something funny is that it is unexpected. Sometimes unexpectedly humorous moments are provided simply by circumstances outside of the teacher's control. Otherwise, constantly facilitating random, funny moments in order to produce more order may seem counter-intuitive. But without bringing that laughter dope, or bringing it in another form such as music or movement - chaos will surely ensue in the direct instruction environment! This is a viable option for those who can facilitate funny to enhance learning.

Movement

The last of the classroom-appropriate doping strategies is movement. Vigorous movement releases endogenous opiates as well, and also serves as an important group bonding mechanism. It is also perhaps the most difficult for teachers to imagine implementing in their subject areas. If a student is moving enough to be breathing hard, they are probably going to be in trouble. Vigorous movement, as well as milder forms of activity, are crucial to learning, memory and creativity – and so the entire next chapter is devoted to the topic of movement.

Summary

In class sizes close to the sympathy group (15), a greater diversity of instructional styles are viable in the classroom, ones that don't require the teacher to maintain order by controlling the floor all of the time. Kids naturally handle the production of laughter, vigorous activity, and music quite readily on their own in such environments. It is just what they do. Therefore, BOTSA-based classroom management strategies are much easier to implement and have greater outcomes within the context of appropriate human social group sizes at school.

As I have attempted to make the case for, the ability of a teacher to facilitate the production of endogenous opiates in student brains is among the most important skills in the classroom. This is especially true as it pertains to classroom management; however, this skill is not a professional teaching standard nor is it an element of teacher training programs.

Teachers should embrace the use of group laughter, music, and movement during instruction to increase group bonding, pain tolerance, positive affect, and ultimately, learning outcomes. Successfully integrating these elements into class sets up a positive feedback loop of intrinsically rewarding pro-social behavior and academic achievement. Now the cat is out of the bag and the catnip is in your hands, teacher!

CHAPTER 9

<u>Ass</u>essments in the Cl<u>ass</u>room: The necessity of movement for learning, memory, and creativity

The dichotomy of body and mind is firmly entrenched in school culture. The body seems to exists for the sole purpose of propping up the head so that it can be properly filled. Whether this is the result of the media through which we learn (paper, monitors, boards, screens, etc.), the need for crowd control, or whatever, it doesn't matter. In this section, I will review evidence showing that students need significantly more physical activity in order to live up to their cognitive, creative, and health potentials. Movement is necessary to stimulate the cellular/molecular gears of learning, as well as to boost creative thinking. It provides a mechanism for social bonding, as well as promotes a positive mood and focused mind for academic success.

Let's first take stock of where we are in terms of youth physical activity levels. Then, we will examine where we need to be. Lastly we will investigate why movement is so important for academic achievement.

The Sit-uation

What if the US Surgeon General placed a large black and white warning sign on the front of our public schools, similar to the warning labels on cigarette packages? It would read something like this:

> **SURGEON GENERAL WARNING:**
> Attending school may increase your risk of cardiovascular diseases such as heart disease or stroke, diabetes, many types of cancer, bone and joint problems, sleep apnea, as well as social and psychological problems.

These are not necessarily maladies of school attendance, but rather, risks for diseases listed by the CDC that stem from obesity.

If you were to follow a typical student throughout his/her school day, it would be hard for one facet to escape your attention: students spend the overwhelming majority of the day sitting still – all day, everyday. The construction of most school furniture will make you painfully aware of this fact after a few hours.

I once had the opportunity to walk in a middle school student's shoes for a day in order to see things from a student's point of view. It is actually more like sitting in a student's pants rather than walking in their shoes, but you get the point.

Going through the paces of a middle school student's schedule, from bell to bell, I clocked a scant 17 minutes on my feet. I earned the largest chunk of time on my toes from racing through lunch. I decided to keep track only because I was in so much discomfort that I started becoming obsessed with time – time until I could stand up, and how little there was of that sort of time during the school day. I spent less than 5% of that school day in light activity such as standing or sauntering to the next class. Despite my experience as a teacher, this was an unexpected and rude awakening – a shocking revelation!

Are schools similar to adult workplaces in regards to activity levels? The Australian workplace study *Stand Up! Australia* (2009) found that office, call center, and retail employees sat over three quarters of the time (77%) – only a couple of the remaining percentage points involved moderate to vigorous levels of movement. The same pattern is evident in schools where youth obesity rates have more than tripled in the past three decades. The CDC reported 17% of children age 2-19 qualified as obese, and an additional 15% were overweight; overall this is about a third of school-aged kids in the United States. However, we shouldn't be sitting around talking about weight without acknowledging the fact that we are sitting down.

For the particular day that I played middle school student, my activity levels at school were markedly less than those of the adults in the *Stand Up! Australia* sedentary workplace study.

Just like I struggled to stay seated all day, kids want to move too. For those kids fortunate enough to have recess scheduled daily, it has become the ultimate punishment/reward tool for behavior management in many schools. Nixing recess is a big hammer. Taking away recess is a popular disciplinary consequence for just about anything, and is frequently imposed on kids who often need the physical activity break the most. After the dismissal bell one day, I watched primary grade school kids walk in a single-file line to the main doors. Three boys burst into a run a step too soon as they hit the doorway. "You just lost your first recess for tomorrow!" trailed a perturbed teacher's voice from behind. For children collectively, recess is in a tenuous position; to the individual kid, recess is always on the line.

American Culture and Obesity

So just what is the result of our sedentary American lifestyles? Perhaps the most striking example of the cultural impact on obesity comes from a study comparing the indigenous Pima populations on each side of the USA/Mexico border (Schultz, 2006). Mexican Pimas live in the remote eastern part of the state of Sonora, a relatively road-less region at the time of the study I will describe. Mexican Pima men get about 33 hours of moderate-to-vigorous physical activity per week, with 22 hours reported for women. In stark contrast, on the USA side of the border, the weekly hours of physical activity were roughly 12 for men and a meager 3 for women. This discrepancy in physical activity resulted in a dramatic difference in health.

You may be wondering how differences in diet affected the outcome. Surprisingly, dietary studies revealed that US Pimas consumed fewer calories than their counterparts south of the border. Yet, a mind-blowing 63.8% of Pima men in the US were obese compared with a mere 6.5% in Mexico. For women, roughly three quarters of US Pimas were obese compared with only one fifth of Mexican Pima women (Schultz, 2006).

The bigger picture conclusion is that our modern American cultural norms, including those practiced in our schools, are severely compromising our health. Even a population with the highest rates of obesity and type-2 diabetes in the world like the Pimas can have a healthy distribution of weights in a more vigorously active environment. Regardless of ethnicity or geography, the conditions that affected Pimas living on the USA side of the border exist everywhere in the USA, from the Redwood forests to the Gulf Stream waters; these are our modern cultural norms. And, as I will argue, the lack of physical activity in our academic institutions is robbing our youth from reaching their academic potential. Let's continue to explore youth physical activity levels in greater depth first.

Youth Activity Levels

In 2009, only 12% of students walked to school, and a meager 1% rode bicycles. Between 1972 and 2011, out of children who lived within one mile (1.6 km) from school, the percentage of K-8 children who walked to school plummeted from 89% to 35%. Commonly cited reasons for not walking or biking to school include: distance, traffic, safety, crime, weather, or school policies (Safe Routes to Schools, 2016). However, the beneficial effects of walking or biking to school extends beyond the commute. Children who walk to school also have higher rates of physical activity outside of school; activity seems to beget more activity.

But what about recess? My own kid's elementary school provides 15 minutes of recess in the morning and again in the afternoon. If a kid can stay out of trouble long enough to participate, surely they will get some activity on the playground! Not necessarily. Eight percent of 3rd graders have never had recess. An additional 15% of 3rd graders received 15 minutes or less of recess time per day (NCES, 2006). The fact that national statistics reveal that nearly a quarter of elementary school kids are getting less than 15 minutes of recess daily is tragic and shocking to me. According to the National Center for Education Statistics, being African American, living below the poverty line, or having below average test scores roughly doubles your chances of not having recess.

The Center on Education Policy (2008) indicated that 20% of schools had cut an average of 50 minutes off of recess time. Schools with students from lower income backgrounds typically lost more recess than their wealthier counterparts. The school district in the city where I reside has about a dozen elementary schools. Even in such a relatively small place, kids would be shocked to learn that their more affluent peers living just a couple of neighborhoods over are getting 100% more recess time (double). Not coincidentally, there is a recess allotment gap facing populations already suffering from achievement gaps. All the while, we have understood this synergistic relationship between vigorous movement and achievement.

CDC Evidence-Based Recommendations Versus the Current Reality

What constitutes an adequate amount of physical activity for youth? The CDC recommends a minimum of 60 minutes of play each day that should consist of moderate to vigorous exercise for young children and adolescents: running, biking, swimming, dancing, etc. A quality PE program with trained instructors is considered a key to achieving these 60 minutes, with recess and out-of-school activities providing the remainder of exercise time. However, the CDC reports in the 2011 national *Youth Risk Behavior Survey* that only 2% of US students participated in daily PE classes for the duration of high school; 69% of students reported that they did not participate in a PE program at all while in high school. Data was not available for elementary schools. My own elementary-age kid has PE once per week for half an hour. PE does not currently appear to provide for much of a child's recommended physical activity needs.

Perhaps the most objective answer to the question of how much activity children actually get comes from the 2013 *Avon Longitudinal Study of Parents And Children* (Boothe, et al, 2011) done in the UK. It showed 11 year-olds getting less than a half hour of moderate to vigorous exercise on average as measured objectively by a hip-worn accelerometer, with girls measuring roughly 60% of that amount – 18 minutes. That is it. That is reality. I will discuss the mental health impacts as well as the effect on academic outcomes later.

As children spend a large portion of the day at school, in-transit, or doing things related to school (such as homework), our education system may be complicit in the obesity and mental health epidemics by not structuring time for physical activity at school. I live at 47° N latitude, which is hardly the North Pole. Yet, for much of the school year, the school day coincides with the limited hours of daylight. After that, it's nothing but darkness, rain, wolves, and zombies. That is why it is essential for school time to include the 1-hour of moderate-to-vigorous exercise recommended by the CDC.

The American Bar Association's (ABA) *Standards on Treatments of Prisoners* (2010) recommends benchmarks for correctional institutions. Among these standards, it sets a minimum baseline for outdoor exercise opportunities for prisoners: Standard 23-3.6 (b) states:

"Each prisoner, including those in segregated housing, should be offered the opportunity for at least one hour per day of exercise, in the open air if the weather permits."

This reflects the CDC's 'one hour' benchmark and should really set the standard for school practice as well, only because it would be embarrassing to not measure up to the guidelines meant for the prison system with regards to humane treatment. Prisons are not granting recreation time purely out of regard for humane treatment towards inmates, but also as an economic matter - to reduce the costs that stem from conflict. The same is true for the impact on the economy of the classroom (Barros, et al, 2009). If elementary school principals started getting advice from prison wardens...

As the world sinks into a global health crisis stemming from a lack of vigorous movement, can we imagine a more healthful future for our children?

Physical Activity in an Evolutionary Context

Instead of looking at a modern day benchmark of physical activity, it is important to answer the question from an evolutionary point of view. How much physical activity have we typically gotten throughout our evolutionary history? It turns out, our human body hardware was meant to move a great deal more for our mental operating system to run effectively.

Evidence that humans evolved the ability to run long distances became popularized in recent years in the book *Born to Run* (McDougall, 2009). We likely evolved this ability, first, to out-compete scavengers and later for persistence hunting – hunting by running down animals to the point of exhaustion. Please excuse the detailed account in the following paragraph, but this is the learning conditions our brains evolved to function in, and this discrepancy with our classroom must be reconciled.

South African Louis Liebenberg, working with San hunter-gathers of the central Kalahari, provided invaluable research at a critical time before this cultural practice was lost forever (Liebenberg 2006). On several persistence hunts, Liebenberg accompanied hunters in their mid-to-late 30's as they tracked antelope in temperatures of 100-and-fuck degrees (38°-42°C, 100°-108°F) through thick brush, on soft sand, for an average of 4 and a half hours, over 28 km (17.3 mi). John Medina, neuroscientist and author of *Brain Rules* (2011), notes that adult male hunter-gatherers covered an average of 12 miles per day. In short, putting a bipedal primate on its butt all day is an insult to that organism's biology.

The quantity of hours of vigorous activity our bodies evolved to handle day-in and day-out may seem like a pie-in-the-sky ideal that only elite endurance athletes would be able to handle. But rather, it is the default level for the common person's brain to function normally. Without a high level of physical activity, we are prone to putting our students' bodies and minds in a diseased state, and rendering ourselves unable to handle the physical and mental challenges of life, school included.

Still Body, Sick Mind

These sedentary times in which we live coincide with an epidemic of mental illness. In his book *Pandora's Seed*, geneticist Spencer Wells remarks that in the 21st Century we take drugs to be normal, with perhaps 40% or more of the population exhibiting symptoms of mental illness.

In Washington State, The *Healthy Youth Survey* is given to students to gauge the health of adolescents and guide public policy. In a 2014 survey, (Figure 6), 10th grade girls from Thurston County, in the State of Washington (home to the capital city of Olympia) reported:

"49% of 10th grade girls in our county felt so sad or hopeless for 2 weeks or more that they stopped doing their usual activities."

Out of the over 1,200 10th grade girls surveyed, nearly one third had considered suicide, and half of those reported actually attempting suicide. The state-wide averages were only slightly lower. Additionally, 83% of those girls surveyed did not meet the minimum recommendation for daily physical activity; 78% were not enrolled in a PE class, and 57% had more than 3 hours of screen time per day.

The *Common Sense Census: Media Use by Tweens and Teens* (Common Sense Media, 2015) revealed an eye-popping average of 9 hours (8:56) of digital media consumption for US teens aged 13-18, and 6 hours (5:55) of media for 8-12 year-olds, excluding screen-time at school and for use on homework! This is indeed the age of mental illness, and poignantly, illness comprises most of the word stillness.

Figure 6. Depression & Suicide in 10th Grade Girls: Results from 2014 WA State Healthy Youth Survey, Thurston County, WA, USA.

Depression & Suicide in 10th Grade Girls

Results from 2014 WA State Healthy Youth Survey (n=1270)
THURSTON CNTY, WASHINGTON, USA

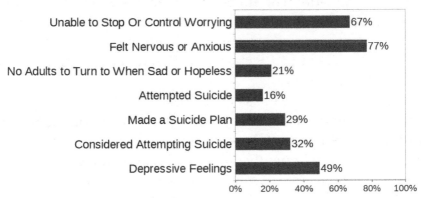

Aerobic exercise can alleviate the symptoms of anxiety and depression, in many cases, as well as prescription drugs. Running operates pharmacologically like many prescription anti-anxiety medications do by boosting the neurotransmitter GABA in the ventral hippocampus (Schoenfeld, 2013). This creates a sense of calm due to the inhibitory action of GABA. Running creates a lot of new and easily excitable neural connections that need to be told to chill out. The calm, focus, and positive mood are a winning combination with the increased learning potential created at the molecular and cellular level by running.

Running provides an impressive buffer against stress and anxiety. Physical activity changes our brain's chemical environment, providing the proper neurochemical marinade for optimal mental performance. This secret sauce is necessary for the brain to focus, persist, learn, and remember at school. To create these conditions, we must provide our brains with the level of physical activity that has been typical over the course of human evolution.

Vigorous Activity and Academic Achievement

We have betrayed our human biology and academic vitality by undermining the relationship between physical activity and cognition. Perhaps it is too counter-intuitive. Perhaps the stereotype of the quiet, un-athletic scholar is so ingrained in our collective minds that we are just missing the mark.

While there have been many studies linking physical activity with academic attainment over the years, these studies have had limitations, such as small sample sizes or non-objective measures of physical activity. However, one study stands out. The *Avon Longitudinal Study of Parents and Children* that I mentioned earlier resulted in a robust study to help solidify the scientific link between academic attainment and physical activity (Boothe, et al, 2013). The study outfitted thousands of 11 year-olds with hip-worn accelerometers and then tracked their performance on national tests at age 11, 13, and 16 in the subjects of mathematics, English, and science.

This large-scale population study with objective measurements seems to have settled the case on the effect of vigorous physical activity on academic attainment. At age 16, student performance on the GSCE (General Certificate of Secondary Education, UK) was predicted by the student's level of moderate to vigorous physical activity measured back when they were 11 years old. Students with the highest levels of physical activity scored better than those with the least activity. Higher levels of activity lead to greater test scores. The increase in moderate to vigorous activity successfully predicted higher test scores across subjects, across ages, and regardless of gender. The data predicted an increase of one letter grade (C to a B, for example) for every 15-minute increase in daily moderate to vigorous physical activity.

It is worth noting again that the average minutes of

moderate to vigorous physical activity by 11 year-olds in the study was only 29 minutes for males, and 18 minutes for females – far below the 1 hour evidence-based recommendations given by CDC health officials.

As with many of the human biology-based interventions throughout this book, exercise tended to benefit those at the bottom of achievement gaps the most. Interestingly, exercise implemented at the small group level seems to show additional benefit. Physical activity helps level the academic playing field and boost achievement for all while not taking away from academics. That is important to reiterate. Exercise interventions do not take away from academics, even when the academic schedule is supplanted for such purposes. Vigorous movement naturally allows students to better capitalize on their own innate mechanisms for learning.

Milder Motion and Creativity

Now that I have emphasized the importance of vigorous aerobic activity like running, we need to turn our attention to the importance of milder levels of physical activity – and what sets it apart from being sedentary as it pertains to the context of school.

I have always held a fascination with the effect that movement has on thinking and creativity. When my young son starts weaving one of his dramatic stories, I notice he always stands up and starts pacing about. You can see similar examples of this type of behavior in other intense pursuits where creativity with language is required. Improvisational actors often appear to be in a hyper-kinetic state while performing, spontaneously giving rise to unexpected funniness. In a Hip Hop cypher, a small circle of emcees groove and gesture along to a simple beat as they take turns creating freestyle rhymes. In each of these pursuits, we see examples where high verbal creativity appears to be aided by mild to moderate levels of movement.

'On Your Toes' for Creativity

A 2014 Stanford study (Oppezzo & Schwartz, 2014) brought researchers one step closer to explaining why people can "think on their feet." These scientists used a "creative divergent thinking test" to compare creativity in walking versus sitting. In this case, what the researchers measured was a participant's ability to produce analogies. The study demonstrated that walking increased 81% of participants' creativity over sitting, with an average increase in creative output of about 60%. People who sat down after walking still showed a short-term lingering boost to their creative output. Walkers were also able to produce more creative analogies than sitters. The connection between creativity and movement is apparent, but what about a neurological mechanism?

Research combining Hip Hop and brain imaging has provided some insight into brain function during these creative situations (Liu, 2012). Scientists hooked up freestyle emcees to functional magnetic resonance imaging (fMRI) machines to analyze their brain activity. fMRI visualizes brain activity by measuring changes in blood flow throughout the brain. Cerebral blood flow and brain activity go hand-in-hand. Rapid blood flow measurements taken by fMRI helped to reveal a glimpse into the possible synaptic origins of creativity itself.

The data (Liu, 2012) showed shifts between parts of the subconscious, where fresh ideas can bubble up, without filter, and the areas of the brain that need to make the idea fit into the world. This pattern of activity in different areas of the brain shifted from the beginning to the end of a musical measure. After starting out in areas that bypassed conscious control, it shifted to the area that constrains the brain's output to the realities of the particular context. Producing a diversity of ideas before narrowing them back down to reality is a well-known divergent thinking exercise for creating innovative solutions. So freestyle rap would seemingly impart an engine of linguistic innovation. I will discuss this mild-motioned language creativity mechanism again when we discuss language arts approaches. And, while we may not be even close to fully understanding neural mechanisms of creativity, it is safe to say that we should keep 'on our toes'.

The cost of sedentary work stations, in terms of productivity, creativity, and health, are driving businesses, government agencies, and elite private schools to rethink the 'norm'. Indeed, in the state office buildings of the Superintendent of Public Instruction, you can find employees who have the option of adjustable 'stand-up' work stations. These types of desks are trickling down from the workplace to classrooms. I once observed a math class where at least half of the kids were bouncing on giant inflated balls which were half their size! There was no detriment to productivity or focus. It is time for us to abandon the myth of the sedentary, quiet, smart child. Children need to move in order to learn, and some more than others. Lack of recess at school should be considered a driver of widening achievement gaps. Rather, recess goes by the wayside in order to try to close stubborn achievement gaps. It's time to put physical and cognitive health in motion for the K-12 masses who are stuck on their seats.

So now that we have the evidence of benefits, let's attempt to interpret it. Why is it that those kids with higher levels of moderate to vigorous activity perform better on school assessments?

Vigorous Movement, Brain-Derived Neurotrophic Factor and the Switchboard of Learning

At the molecular/cellular level, vigorous exercise stimulates the neurological groundwork needed for learning and memory. Brain-Derived Neurotrophic Factor, BDNF for short, is a protein that stimulates synaptic plasticity in the hippocampus. Synaptic plasticity is the reorganization of connections (synapses) between neurons in the brain. This plasticity, or change-ability, refers to when synapses build and lose connections as we learn. You can envision this as a switchboard turning connections on and off. BDNF allows the hippocampal neurons to make new connections, diversify connections, increase the bandwidth of important connections, and drop irrelevant ones.

Rats (Vaynman, et al, 2004) that are allowed to run produce higher levels of BDNF than rats that sit around all day. Scientists looked for BDNF expressed in the hippocampus, a dynamic area of the brain best known for its role in learning and memory in rats (as well as humans). The running rats had significantly higher BDNF levels (as well as chemicals working under its direction). But did these higher BDNF levels result in better learning? Yes! The exercising rats performed much better on learning and memory tests such as the Morris Swim Maze. It probably isn't how you would picture a maze. It's essentially a rat-sized swimming pool with a hidden platform where the rat can stand. Rats who ran, but had their BDNF chemically blocked, performed the maze at the same level as rats who had no exercise. This underscores the role of BDNF in exercise-induced learning and memory enhancement (Figure 7).

So the question is, why wouldn't we want our students making more of this exercise-stimulated BDNF stuff if it significantly enhances learning and memory? Perhaps a 5 kilometer jog or dancing wildly to a handful of tunes would do better for cognition than 30 minutes of mundane busy work. In reality, learning and exercise work together to enhance academic ability. A school with a DEAR program (Drop Everything And Read) will likely perform significantly better if it were to also schedule a 'Drop Everything And Run' program.

Figure 7. Outcomes Stemming from Changes to the Brain due to Vigorous Exercise

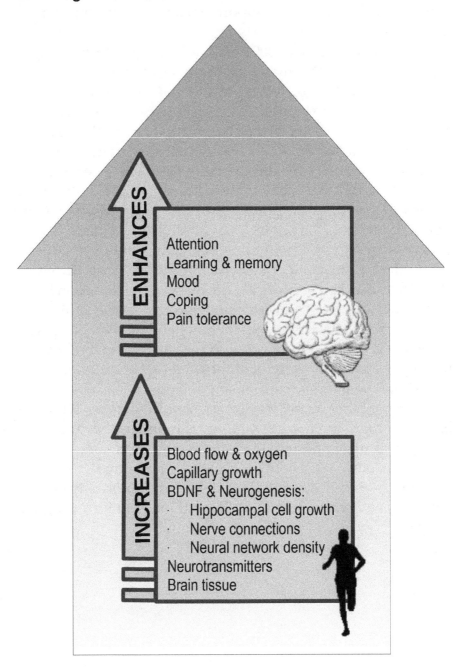

Hippocampal Double Jeopardy

Students who face additional stress in life, including school itself, face double jeopardy from the idle conditions of school. The hippocampus is especially rich in receptors for stress hormones. Stress negatively affects the hippocampus, and inhibits learning as a result. Vigorous movement is one way to help mitigate stress, though there is little opportunity for vigorous movement at school, and vigorous activity is not often accomplished by youth outside of the school day. For the extra-stressed students who lack vigorous movement, this is a recipe for an achievement gap. Vigorous movement would stimulate BDNF levels and decrease stress hormones, elevating both learning and memory. Higher levels of movement would reverse these two negative conditions into positive factors for cognition.

Unfortunately, schooling was never really designed to hit a moving target. From our classroom infrastructure to our instructional methods, the pedagogy is geared towards a physically incapacitated learning orientation. A great paradigm shift is in order with regard to vigorous movement at school.

Drop Everything and Run (Summary)

In today's school culture, exhibiting truly normal human behavior as it has been characterized since the dawning of our species is viewed as disorderly and deviant. Our kids are disciplined and drugged into the sit-down, sit-still for seven hours model and it is time for the great stationary schooling experiment to go extinct. As the persistence hunter example illustrated, the heights of scientific practice can be achieved while chasing antelope through the desert. Not only can it be done, this is how our body evolved to do it. So why is a wiggly kid such an abomination to the learning process? We must reorient our educational practice along this standard. However, teachers simply were never trained to develop lesson plans geared towards students moving at 10 km/hour.

Until we re-imagine what teaching and learning looks like at human speed, we will continue to suffer the cognitive, social, emotional, physical, and mental health consequences. If we want our academically struggling students to perform better in the great race of school achievement, we have to stop shooting them in the foot at the starting line. Our current education environment ironically works to impede the body's own biological engine of creativity, learning, and memory. When school policies restrict natural levels of movement by students, they ironically put schools at odds with fulfilling their educational potentials.

CHAPTER 10

The Ecology Of Special Needs Students: Making the most of the cognitive diversity in the school gene pool

When our school environment undermines the performance of typical functioning students, it certainly impacts kids with special needs. While special education services provide accommodations, they often do not rectify the underlying incongruity of schooling to juvenile human biology. However, once a proper foundation is laid, the conditions are right for a more inclusive environment where fewer accommodations may be needed in the first place.

As sophisticated as our material culture becomes, under the hood, we humans are still made of hunter-gatherer gear. We have been providing evidence for why we should remodel our school environment to take advantage of such ancient human hardware. In this section, I will explain how viewing schools through an evolutionary framework can, in essence, provide a blanket accommodation that not only helps typical students, but gives an extra boost to their special needs peers. We will examine two prevalent conditions that challenge teachers: ADHD and Autism Spectrum Disorder. We will investigate these disorders and how they relate to school from an evolutionary point of view.

As we will learn, these special needs were not born in the modern era. The primary genes responsible for these disorders evolved over thousands and thousands of years with the rest of our genome. I will explain how we can help special needs students thrive by modifying our school environment to better resemble the environment of our hunter-gatherer ancestors.

ADHD

Our first stop will be the one-kid-wrecking-crew with behaviors known as Attention Deficit Hyperactivity Disorder (ADHD). ADHD represents the roughly 5-10% of people who are at the upper-end of the continuum of hyperactivity, impulsiveness, and inattention. In 2011, 8% of children overall and 12% of boys were estimated to have ADHD (Eisenberg & Campbell, 2011). ADHD is often perceived as a late-20th century epidemic, something that didn't exist before modern psychiatric definitions, pharmaceuticals, and standardized testing.

However, ADHD has a high heritability. At least 75% of the effects can be attributed to genetics (Rietveld, 2004 and Faraone, et al, 2005), and those genes have been passed down for millennia upon millenia. The real story of ADHD goes way back – and the cognitive diversity it bestows turns out to be one of the major themes in our human story of survival and adaptability. Before we examine this trait in the classroom, let's take a look at how ADHD came to be in this world.

ADHD Origins

Roughly 40-50,000 years ago, a rare genetic mutation occurred in a dopamine receptor gene (Chang, 1996). When this happened, the course of humanity on our planet was forever changed. But before we get into the nitty-gritty details, it's important to understand that the dopamine receptor gene we are talking about (DRD4-4R) is old – on the order of 300,000 years-old. This would make it older than our *Homo sapiens* species (Ding, 2001). The mutation that occurred changed DRD4-4R into DRD4-7R, otherwise known as the 'ADHD allele' (an allele is simply a different version of a gene). Although ADHD may involve several dopamine-related genes and environmental factors, we now understand this DRD4-7R 'ADHD allele' to be associated with ADHD (Gizer, et al, 2010;

Faraone, et al, 2005; Swanson, 1998).

The attention-lacking, hyperactive, and impulsive behaviors of ADHD have their roots in dopamine neurochemistry. The ADHD allele codes for a dopamine receptor that doesn't function as well. Therefore, ADHD individuals require more dopamine to achieve the same base-line state as the typical functioning version of the receptor. ADHD kids may need a greater amount of stimulation to achieve those higher dopamine levels (Wang, 2004). A persistent neurological quest for stimulation leads to the behaviors we associate with attention-deficit kids.

Genetic evidence suggests that the ADHD allele most likely arose somewhere in Africa prior to the last major human migration out of Africa (Chang, et al, 1996), which occurred roughly 40,000 – 80,000 years ago (Cambell & Tishkoff, 2010). Human culture flourished in the following era. With a new-found diversity of replicable ideas to choose from (or knowing what to avoid), adaptation to new environments could theoretically have proceeded more easily.

There may have been positive natural selection for ADHD genetics (Matthews, et al, 2011). For whatever reason, people who had these ADHD versions of the gene survived and left behind more offspring. People with ADHD genetics may have been more likely to pioneer the settlement of a new environment and cope with its stresses. We see higher rates of the ADHD allele in places furthest away from our common African homeland, and in peoples with histories of successive migrations, such as in the Americas.

Does ADHD help humans survive times of rapid change? Could the ADHD allele be, in part, responsible for the successful proliferation and spread of humans for the past 50,000 years? Let's take a look.

ADHD Genetics and Environment

When we look outside of our sedentary, modern-day

society, can we find benefits of ADHD? One day, a headline about attention deficit pastoral nomads from east Africa caught my eye (Eisenberg, 2008). What really caught my eye first was the photo of a man that accompanied the article. The man seemed to have the same look in his eye as the ADHD kid in one of my morning classes. The man from the study was from the Ariaal people, who have traditionally carried out their pastoral lives out in the desert of remote northern Kenya. Their relative isolation have made the Ariaal sought-after subjects of study time and time again.

One measure of success in a chronically undernourished population is having a higher body mass index (BMI). By examining the ADHD-related allele, Eisenberg (2008) was able to compare the effects of ADHD of the traditional nomadic Ariaal with those Ariaal who had settled and were living a more sedentary lifestyle.

The Ariaal still living as camel herders who had the ADHD allele had a higher BMI than nomads without it. In other words, the attention-deficit herders were able to put on weight more successfully. There was an interesting finding amongst the Ariaal's recently settled counterparts as well. The settled Ariaal who had the ADHD allele had lower BMI's than their settled counterparts without the mutation (Eisenberg, 2008). In the case of settled populations, the gene associated with ADHD appears to be a handicap. This settled environ may be more similar to our present school setting, and the struggle was apparent in the waistline.

The meaning of this research from a remote part of the globe is clear: In order for children with attention deficit disorder to thrive, they must seek the vocational path of a hungry shepherd. Just kidding – but not entirely. The real inspiration from this research is the importance of the interplay of the ADHD allele and the environment. It begs the question of whether or not our schools can be the environment where a child with ADHD genetics can thrive.

Can there be an advantage to having ADHD in the

classroom? After all, ADHD provided for the day-to-day success that allowed nomadic pastoral tribesman in arid northern Kenya to carry some extra flesh on their lean frames. Perhaps as handicapping as ADHD can be in our 21st century schools, ADHD may be more advantageous in an environ more closely akin to the one where ADHD genetics originated and multiplied.

ADHD as Knowledge-Seeking Behavior

Society generally views ADHD from a negative perspective. We can change this mindset if we look at ADHD through an evolutionary lens. ADHD is labeled as a dis-order; however, ADHD is a disorder that nature seems to like for some particular reason. Scientists who have studied ADHD genes and their behaviors (Williams & Taylor, 2006) redefine the behavior like this:

> "Specifically, we re-frame DRD4-7R's effect, and more generally ADHD–HI's* [*High-Impulsivity], as not merely novelty-seeking and risk-taking for its own sake, but for exploratory knowledge acquisition."

Populations indigenous to the Americas have the highest ratio of the ADHD allele in the world (Ding, 2002). This allele may have helped to enable the rapid exploration and survival in the New World, from the arctic to the antarctic, seal blubber to quinoa. We may never know who was the first person to step foot in the lands we now call the Americas, but my bet is on an ADHD individual.

Our schools' grudge with ADHD is due to a misunderstanding. Any standardized test that can be evaluated efficiently and profitably is likely not going to value clever, innovative solutions or new ideas – nor the mistakes and messes that come from such learning. In the content-based standards and assessment craze, there appears to be diminishing value for knowledge gained through exploration or innovation. Additionally, our overpopulated classrooms and schools have placed a premium on order, control, and discipline. The acquisition of knowledge through experience, which may often be impulsive and relatively unpredictable, is too often viewed as deviant.

If we can begin to view ADHD as knowledge-seeking behavior, certainly we can do better at leveraging the benefits of this behavior at school. Knowledge and school sound like they should be compatible, don't they?

Individual and Social Learning Benefits of ADHD

In computer simulations (Williams & Taylor, 2006), hunter-gather scale populations composed of 5-10% ADHD individuals did better surviving periods of simulated diet changes over evolutionary time. In this era of unprecedented, rapid environmental change, perhaps this diversity of thought will lead to discoveries that can help us meet the challenges of an uncertain future. Without ADHD, there will be fewer boundaries pushed, fewer novel discoveries and explorations made, and less information revealed (Williams and Taylor, 2006) – both for the student, and by social context, for the class.

Reaping the Rewards and Mitigating the Damage of ADHD

ADHD has been described as a plastic trait. Just as plastic can bend and mold under the right conditions, the degree to which an individual exhibits ADHD behaviors can change depending on the situation. When the environment changes, perhaps to a more stressful one, the genetic prerequisites combine with the environmental conditions to spring forth exaggerated ADHD behaviors. This may allow new information to be discovered during times of stress. Unfortunately, these stressful conditions emerge in the classroom. Revealing new knowledge during crucial times in the past, may have lead to better survival, but do not lead to success in the classroom. So, where to we go from here? We go outside.

Modifying the school environment to meet the needs of ADHD kids will likely give an extra boost to typical kids as well. Research on recreation interventions done in green, natural environments indicates that these settings reduce ADHD symptoms and the need for medication (Kuo, 2004). Functional Magnetic Resonance Imaging (fMRI) has allowed us to visualize increased blood flow to areas of the brain responsible for executive function and rule acquisition during such outdoor recreation periods. More blood flow to these areas tells us that the brain is better able to control behavior and understand boundaries. While few classrooms operate outside, this research highlights the importance of outdoor recreation as a therapy for ADHD individuals. Time spent exercising outdoors can reduce ADHD behavior when the student is back in the classroom.

We've talked a lot about the importance of class size to student success. With ADHD students, it may be important to limit the total number of ADHD students in a single class. At a 5-10% ADHD prevalence rate in youth, statistically, there are 1.5 to 3 students with ADHD in a single classroom of 30 kids. My experience tells me that the prevalence as a percentage isn't as important to the classroom as the number of ADHD kids supervised by one teacher contained between one set of walls. Having more than one individual with ADHD in the same room may provide too much relatively unpredictable behavior to manage and perhaps the potential benefits to the group and individual are lost in the chaos. However, with a class size of 15, there would statistically be .75 to 1.5 ADHD students per class – which translates to one, sometimes two per class.

With only one ADHD kid to manage, benefits flow from that child's accidents, mistakes, impulses, boundary pushing, and discoveries. Compelled by curiosity that is equipped with faulty brakes, ADHD students can be a runaway Pandora's Box of new information, bodily injury, property damage, and social disruption. One ADHD individual per 1000 square feet should be enough. Or, in the case of outdoor environments, one ADHD individual per sympathy group should be enough. Even without walls, there is a sweet spot in the ratio of novelty to predictability in students that can be crafted by class size. That one ADHD kid will be a prolific source of diverse actions to choose winning ideas from, and also show others what dangers to avoid.

ADHD, Drugs, and the Academic Environment

We will close this section where we often end up with ADHD in our society: drugs. While the human race still desperately needs novel and innovative thinking, the modern school is woefully inept at meeting that need. The volume of typical, non-ADHD students using illegal ADHD drugs is a testament to this. In 2004-5, (DeSantis & Webb, 2008) 34% of students at a large research university in the southern United States reported that they had used ADHD prescription stimulants illegally, primarily during periods of high academic stress. ADHD stimulants increase dopamine levels in the brain. This helps those with less functional dopamine receptors function normally by increasing dopamine concentrations. It also enhances the concentration and studying abilities of more typical students coping with sensory-depriving academic environments. This exemplifies the ill fit of schooling to the biology of a typical Little Homo Sapiens, but even more so if ADHD genetics are present.

While difficult to manage, it is important to view ADHD children for the learning opportunities that they offer the class and themselves. Let's acknowledge the benefits and pitfalls of having ADHD. Let's follow the pattern in nature that has confined attention deficit hyperactivity disorder behaviors to a small percentage of the population. By keeping class sizes proximal to sympathy group sizes, and therefore an average of one ADHD kid per class, we can reap the rewards ADHD offers while mitigating the physical and social damage. Let's learn non-stop from our ADHD students by keeping them managed in as small of numbers as possible. As a courtesy and a thanks for shouldering the risks, we can help to keep them from removing themselves from the gene pool, or ending up in the ER, while in pursuit of knowledge. With human-scaled schools, students have more interpersonal knowledge of their ADHD peers, which helps everyone to work better together. Greening up the educational environment along with outdoor physical activity may allow ADHD students to reduce disruptive behaviors and thrive. The good news is that when we use these principles to design a school where ADHD Little Homo Sapiens can thrive, the design benefits typical students as well.

ADHD In Summary

- ADHD adds cognitive diversity through novelty and knowledge seeking behavior, and impulsivity.

- The ADHD behaviors listed above are influenced by environment. Natural 'green' environments seem to reduce ADHD behaviors.

- ADHD genes may spark knowledge-seeking behavior that both individuals, and their peers, can benefit from.

- Confining risk to a limited number of people helps keep the group safe, while allowing everyone to benefit from the new knowledge and the ability to replicate successful strategies.

- ADHD genes must be maintained in lower frequencies to manage the chaos.

Autism Spectrum Disorder: Genetics & Evolution

Schools often have wall decor that exalt the value of diversity in learning. We have demonstrated that cognitive diversity, the different thinking and actions of ADHD individuals, can be of value to both the individual and by social context, everyone in the group. But, perhaps there is no greater cognitive diversity than that possessed by kids with Autism Spectrum Disorders (known by the acronym ASD). ASD students are characterized by substantial social, behavioral, and communication challenges. ASD can result in exceptionally high cognitive abilities as well.

Autism is an evolutionary riddle: What kind of disease is passed on through genes, but the disease results in low reproductive success for the offspring? Would that not put an end to the passing on of the genes? Wouldn't natural selection bring about a quick demise to such genetics? From an evolutionary perspective, scientists can explain how Autism (ASD) counter-intuitively makes total sense (Ploeger and Galis, 2011).

Autism is a polygenic disorder. Polygenic disorders are determined by several different genes; in the case of Autism, at least 30 different genes, which interact (Ploeger and Galis, 2011). The same genes that result in Autism are also known for their developmental role in conferring intelligence. There has been positive selection for brainy genes in our species. Most of the time, the result is typical human intelligence.

However, unfortunate interactions of genes during brain development can sometimes result in Autism Spectrum Disorder characteristics. For example, a copy of a gene from the father might 'silence' the copy of the gene from the mother. This biochemical 'silencing' can make things difficult if detrimental mutations to genes underlying Autism have spontaneously popped up and are passed on to the offspring. If, for example, a 'good' functional gene from mom gets silenced, only the dysfunctional one from the father will be expressed.

Because intelligence is nothing new to humans, Autism Spectrum Disorder is likely not just a new diagnosis, but rather characteristics of individuals in our communities throughout modern human existence. Once again, we will turn to the ancient hunter-gatherer context for answers. There are no easy solutions to this issue, and some readers may find my lone solution oversimplified. However, it is what I have found currently works best for ASD students amongst the general population, and it is the same thing that works for every other student. Aside from specific therapies, interventions, and ongoing research and advocacy on a variety of fronts, I want to discuss ASD from a bigger picture perspective. As I have mentioned before, it is the most vulnerable students who suffer from conflicts between human evolution and school design; they also gain the most when the problem is rectified. We are now going to take an ASD student named Little Homo Sapiens back to his clan.

Autism Spectrum Disorders and Cognitive Diversity: Knowledge of the individual in a social context

Autism advocacy organizations (see Autismspeaks.org, for example) have recommendations for teachers as to how to make their classrooms more ASD-friendly. Of primary importance is the crucial thematic recommendation that students with ASD really be considered as individuals. Therefore, in looking to deal with this complex condition at school, I will focus on the ASD student as one having needs that need to be understood on the individual level. Because 'no student is an island', we will focus on the individual through the lens of the cognitive group: individual knowledge in a fitting social context.

If highly individualized instruction is required for ASD students to thrive, detailed knowledge of what works and doesn't work is important not only to the teacher, but for classmates as well. It is important to understand what ASD students' motivations and preferences are, as they may have specific interests and particular ways of doing things. A teacher (and fellow students) must know where to meet that student in terms of social skill development, as well as with coursework and communication ability.

Humans have roamed the planet in small, largely egalitarian groups for most of our existence. We would have surely possessed detailed reciprocal knowledge of each other's life histories, behaviors, social thinking, communication abilities, social skill development, motivations, talents and skills, etc. This is no longer the case, especially in our middle and high schools. I suggest that proper integration of ASD students into the academic fabric of our schools is predicated on a return to the type of social setting and group sizes that humans experienced throughout our evolutionary history.

The amount of insight into an ASD student's mind needed to provide individualized instruction may not be possible to achieve beyond the cognitive group size of around 150. Time constraints and brain limitations are going to limit the extent to which educators can customize a program that is effective for the ASD student. That is no slight on educators, it just reflects a human biological limit. Likewise, classmates may not have enough background knowledge to engage successfully with the student, leaving conditions ripe for that student to be left by the wayside – subject to stereotype amidst a socially stressful environment. Social skills that work sufficiently between typical-functioning peers may not yield any traction with ASD students. This results in unrealized academic and social growth for the ASD student. It also reduces the likelihood that classmates will benefit from the cognitive diversity in their midst.

The precise prevalence of ASD has been a little uncertain. The CDC lists the prevalence rate of 1 in 68 for 2010 (about 1.5%), more than twice what it was a decade prior. A 2011 South Korean study of over 55,000 students ages 7-12 (Kim, et al. 2011) found a 2.64% prevalence rate. That is 1 in 38, with two-thirds of the ASD students in that country being identified in the general population – undiagnosed and outside of current special education services. Even if we use the higher prevalence rate from South Korea, we are statistically looking at roughly one kid per band at most, or a few per cognitive group.

For the well-being of ASD students, it is recommended that teachers maintain neat and orderly surfaces and rooms. However, a classroom with 30 kids is its own inherent clutter: sights, sounds, stuff, interactions, etc. This may be enough for those ASD students with sensory processing difficulties to be stressed to the point of not functioning effectively. This is the default public school setting and it is at odds with the main 'individualize' recommendation set out at the beginning of this ASD section.

I strongly believe, and have learned from my own teaching experience, that those 'individual' needs of ASD students can be directly, yet passively addressed by the framework in this text. Appropriate, evolutionary, human-scaled group sizes are essential for knowing individuals beyond stereotype. Beyond that, we really need to be able to read the ASD student's mind pretty well in order to help them succeed. Additionally, working within the hierarchy of evolutionary human group sizes makes the ambient sensory conditions more manageable for ASD students.

This human group size framework provides a blanket accommodation that helps everyone, yet benefits those with special needs the most. A teacher (and fellow students) can know where to meet that ASD student in terms of social skill development, as well as with coursework ability and communication. In this sense, the entire system is contributing to enhancing the social and academic success of the student, rather than primarily the teacher and special education support staff. Additionally, others can benefit from the cognitive diversity bestowed by ASD.

CHAPTER 11

First Period Narcolepsy Convention: Waking up to adolescent sleep phase delay

A growing chorus of scientists, medical professionals, parents, and educators have been adding their voices to the push for later, more appropriate high school start times (Adolescent Sleep Working Group, 2014). It is perhaps the most obvious example of biological incompatibility with a school norm and has gained widespread attention from the general public. This is largely due to the advocacy of researchers who are compelled to change the paradigm based on the shocking nature of their findings. While there are many cultural and administrative barriers to making later school start times a reality for teens, the focus of this text is on the science, and what is the best fit given that information.

The Problem

I once taught a high school chemistry class that started at 7:15 am. I might as well have been the keynote speaker at a convention for narcoleptics. A study of 10th-graders revealed that they fell asleep quite readily during an 8:30 am sleep test (Carskadon, et al, 1998). Nearly half fell quickly into the REM sleep associated with dreams in just under three and a half minutes – behavior that mimics the clinical characteristics of narcolepsy. While narcolepsy is a rare and serious neurological disorder, high school students simply suffer from poor school scheduling.

For students in their teenage years, there is no such thing as great teaching during the 7 o'clock or even 8 o'clock hours. The same lessons that are great during third period, flop during first period – Every. Single. Day. I found that no degree of adaptation can make learning more effective during these early hours. The mental fog of "pathological sleepiness" is simply too thick. A case study using freshman at the US Air Force Academy (Carell, et al, 2010) showed that changing start times by 50 minutes resulted in the equivalent of raising teacher quality by 1 standard deviation. That means that if the teacher was totally average, (the #50th best teacher out of 100), delaying start times by about an hour would magically have the same effect on students as being taught by the #16th best teacher. However, the teacher never changed here - that is just how thick the fog is!

In Wake County, NC, an enrollment boom forced the school district to vary middle school start times because they had to share the same buses (Edwards, 2011). Noteworthy gains were made when the morning start bell rang one hour later. They also showed something that I have brought up repeatedly: When you rectify a biological conflict with school, disadvantaged students gain disproportionately more. In this case, twice as much (Jacob & Rockoff, 2011) as kids who could afford their own lunch.

I've seen less than mediocre academic performances turn brilliant (and vice versa) simply by moving students into a class three hours later in the morning. To make matters worse, case studies reveal that the damage done during first period doesn't stay in first period (Carell, et al, 2010); student performance is adversely affected throughout the entire class schedule for typical secondary school start times. Let's take a look at the scientific research for clarity on the issue.

Melatonin is a component of the circadian rhythm – the day/night, wake/sleep cycle in humans. Melatonin causes us to feel sleepy and lowers our core body temperature. Melatonin release is blocked during the daytime when high-energy blue wavelengths of light from the sun are detected by the retina in the back of your eye. In the evening, melatonin begins to be released into the bloodstream from the pineal gland as weaker red wavelengths of light predominate. Electric household lighting and fires give off a low amount of melatonin-inhibiting blue wavelengths compared with natural daylight, so these sources don't interfere much with melatonin production.

In teens (Carskadon, 1998), the secretion of melatonin is delayed in the evening, and the peak persists much later into the morning than we see in adults and young children. This means that teens are on a natural 'late to bed, late to rise' cycle (Carskadon, 1993). Melatonin can be detected in saliva, and this makes it relatively easy to detect experimentally. Research involving 10th graders (Carskadon, 1998) shows that they start releasing melatonin in response to dim light upwards of 9 pm. They typically start sleeping around a quarter to 11 pm. Their peak melatonin production is about 7 am in the morning, and given the opportunity to wake up spontaneously without an alarm, they will rise sometime during the 8' o'clock hour on average. (Please see Figure 8). The peak of melatonin release in the morning is just prior to when the start bell rings at your typical high school.

This creates a huge sleep dilemma on school nights. Teens are biologically programmed to sleep in. Their peak melatonin production is naturally an hour after their alarm has sounded at 6 am. Research shows that teens need at least 9.2 hours of sleep to function properly, while most get less than 7 (Keyes, 2015). This results in chronic sleep deficits. 'Early-to-bed, early-to-rise' is a nice saying, but biologically futile for teens. They are not biologically driven to sleep until much later at night. This whole phenomenon is referred to as adolescent sleep phase delay. Let's take a deeper look at why sleep is necessary in the first place.

Figure 8. Average sleep / wake cycles of 16 year-olds on school nights and non-school nights compared with a more optimal pattern. (Based on data from Carskadon, 1998).

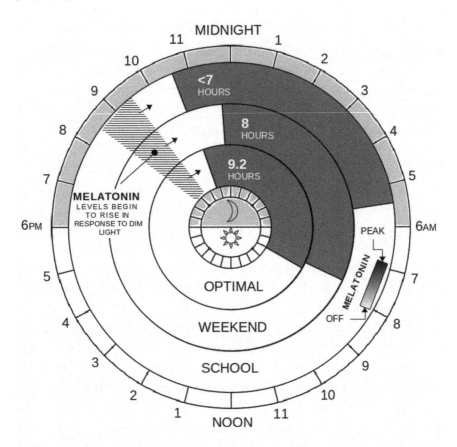

Sleep: Learning & Memory

Sleep has been shown to play a necessary role in the learning process. Conventional wisdom tells us to 'sleep on it' when we have taken in a lot of new information or when facing a difficult decision. In Figure 9 below, a model of how memories come to be over time (Walker, 2005) helps to explain the role of sleep in learning (Figure 9).

Figure 9. Model of Memory Formation Over Time (based on info in Walker, 2005).

Memory Formation Over Time

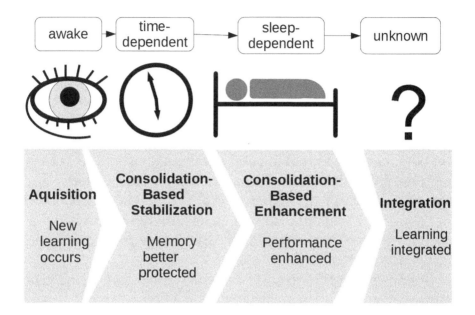

The first step is acquisition, in which a new behavior is done for the first time. Within the next six hours, without further practice, the memory is consolidated and stabilized. You won't perform any better or worse after this time, but the memory is better protected. Next comes the interesting part as far as sleep is concerned. A sleep-dependent consolidation step takes place that enhances your ability to retain the information. By simply sleeping on it, you can improve the learned behavior and perform better than where you left off after the initial skill acquisition. The memory is then further integrated into our neural networks.

Scientists have observed exactly how sleep enhances memory consolidation at the molecular level (Frank, et al, 2009). This research comes from examining kittens who wore a single eye patch – like pirates. These pirate kitties were still actively developing the connections in their visual cortex, that is to say, their brains were still learning how to see. Piracy is treacherous work, and while I can't say that no feline buccaneers were harmed during this research, the study yielded treasure.

When you learn something for the first time, your brain creates new pathways of neurons. While you are asleep, these same neurons are reactivated, and a series of enzymes begins the processes of reorganizing these neural networks. Learning can be thought of as making and breaking connections between neurons in the brain; this reorganization process (called synaptic plasticity) strengthens the appropriate connections. In the case of our swashbuckling mousers, there was probably a steep learning curve while the cat was awake and learning how to function with one eye.

Scientists found molecular evidence of learning in the visual pathways of eye-patch wearing kittens who had slept. This was not observed in the brains of control cats that did not wear eye patches or did not sleep (Frank, et al, 2009).

Science has demonstrated that sleep plays an important role in learning. While early start times may be considered a normal part of high school, they lead to chronic sleep debt and are clearly out of sync with teen biology. The damage this has on the learning process is so clear, it can no longer be ignored.

Dirty Mind Clean-Up

The large sign in front of the gas station down the street reminds patrons that energy drinks are 'EBT Card Approved.' Sleep deprivation is so widespread in our culture that the Centers for Disease Control classified insufficient sleep as a public health epidemic. There are various suspects in this epidemic – from 24 hour access to social media to graveyard work shifts. Whatever the cause, it is clear that Americans are over-caffeinated and under-slept. Teenagers, especially girls, may be suffering the most. Researchers from Columbia University (Keyes, et al, 2015) surveyed teenagers from 1991-2012 and found that over the past 20 years, teens are getting progressively less sleep, with the large majority of teens getting less than 7 hours per night.

In a technological world that never sleeps, the idea of doing nothing for 8 hours or more may seem like an apparent waste of time. It is important, however, not to view sleep as 'unproductive' time. Sleep is not as passive of an activity as it might seem. My pre-schooler loves to play more than he likes to pick-up, but we know that we must build-in time for cleaning up, and make it a priority. This is the same perspective that we must take with the brain. In 2013, sleep scientists (Xie, et al, 2013) found that our brains are too busy to clean-up during waking hours; our brains are so busy processing that there is little energy available for simultaneous cleaning. Just like pre-schoolers busy at play, a mess accumulates that must be dealt with eventually. Fortunately for us, the brain clean-up happens while we sleep. Unless we aren't getting enough.

Glial cells surround neurons in the brain and perform many vital support functions. Recent research on mice shows that while sleeping, cerebral spinal fluid is transported through a network of channels in the glia, and toxic metabolic waste products are removed from the brain in this manner. These channels expanded by 60% while mice slept (Xie, et al, 2013). Pumping cerebral spinal fluid across a cell membrane takes a relatively large amount of energy. This explains why it can't be done as effectively when the mice are awake and sensory processing is consuming much of the available energy. Amyloid proteins that form plaques associated with Alzheimer's Disease are an example of some of the waste products removed during sleep. Sleep plays a critical, restorative role in removing accumulated waste from the brain.

School Start Times: The big payback

In 2011, researchers (Jacob & Rockoff, 2011) did an economic analysis of delaying middle and high school times by 1 hour. This was measured in overall lifetime earnings. They found a benefit/cost ratio of at least 9:1. To put this simply, the cost of delaying start times for these students by 1 hour would generate nine times more than that cost in future wages. With a 1-hour later start time, test scores increased by an average of .175 standard deviations, with disadvantaged students showing the greatest (double) gains. In an era of declining funding, when we are trying to get the biggest bang for our education buck, doesn't it seem strange that we still throw away a decent percentage of every day due to sleepiness? By simply delaying start times, we could see dramatic increases in student achievement and healthier sleep habits as well.

I once taught at a small public high school that started mid-afternoon and ended at 8:40 pm. It was a second shift for the campus of a traditionally scheduled high school. Many students reportedly had the opportunity to awaken spontaneously, without the aid of an alarm or parent. It was certainly the most alert group of high school students that I have ever been able to work with. This experience really got me thinking about the hours of day that schooling takes place.

Regardless of barriers to change, schools are complicit in the promotion of improper sleep habits through administrative decision-making that is irrespective of adolescent biology. The costs to learning are significant (Jacob & Rockoff, 2011). Academics aside, chronic sleep deprivation in teens is related to increases in car accidents, depression, ADHD and other mood/psychological disorders, weight gain, and increased susceptibility to drug and alcohol abuse.

School start times or homework routines that interfere with sleep are counter-productive to learning. The adolescent sleep phase delay aspect of teen biology will not change no matter how long we keep ringing the start bell during the 8 o'clock hour or earlier. Schools can either modify their bell and bus schedules to harmonize with students' natural sleep cycles, or they can remain in conflict with teen biology – and realize the large costs associated with that conflict. It is a conflict which disproportionately affects a disadvantaged Little Homo Sapiens. Let's let science inform the remedy for her sake.

To summarize, sleep is a biological necessity that our school environments must address in order to be effective. Sleep is required for cleansing accumulated toxic waste products from the brain. Sleep is also the time when learning is enhanced by remodeling and strengthening the pathways of neurons that are activated while learning during the day. To put it simply, teens need later school start times. They need as much sleep as younger kids but they are biologically driven to sleep or wake on a delayed schedule.

PART IV
Breaking the Mental Chains

CHAPTER 12

Stereotype Threat and San-Sational Science Stories: Re-framing academics to reduce achievement gaps

Negative academic stereotypes are a new thing in the human social-scape. Because humans roamed the planet in small, egalitarian, hunter-gatherer bands for most of our evolutionary history, everyone we encountered would have been known as an individual. We evolved in a world free of race and racism, mass media, reading, writing, and schools. Therefore, it is unlikely that our brain specifically evolved to be sensitive to stereotypes, let alone negative academic stereotypes attributed to race, class, etc.

Of greater consequence is the fact that negative stereotypes affect our need to protect our reputations in insidious ways. Our reputation in the community is of high importance to each of us and essential for each of us to thrive (Emler, 1992). A brain wired for reputation management fulfills a primal evolutionary function of our social nature. Reputation management is a fundamentally human characteristic that has surely followed us into the digital age. Companies will manage your reputation (or that of a corporate identity) in cyberspace for a price. Our craniums are fundamentally rigged up to detect and deal with all the second-hand social information going around. So it may come as no surprise that I will claim that this reputation management function of our brains is partly to blame for one of the most intractable issues to haunt education in America: The dreaded achievement gaps.

Stereotype Threat

In 1995, J. Aronson and Claude Steele (Steele, 2010) came up with the term "stereotype threat" to describe what they had observed in a series of experiments. They observed that African American men, for whom negative academic stereotypes are pervasive, performed significantly worse on exams when they were made aware of their identity prior to taking the test. Aronson and Steele (1995) originally defined stereotype threat as "being at risk of confirming, as self-characteristic, a negative stereotype about one's group." In other words, simply drawing attention to a person's demographics – (female, teenager, Latina, Pacific Islander, etc.) allows the prevailing negative stereotypes to get into the person's head and undermine their ability to perform. This phenomenon has been experimentally replicated *ad infinitum* for a large diversity of groups, which indicates that stereotype threat is universal. Stereotype threat helps to partially explain discrepant patterns of school performance for those at the bottom of the achievement gap.

How does stereotype threat hurt academic performance? According to the theory, our brains become so busy trying to refute the negative stereotype, that we tie up limited brain power needed to perform up to our potential. When we fail to perform, the stereotype is confirmed – everything society told us we couldn't do, we now can't do. What happens when this level of daily stress is compounded over years? We know how that story ends.

In the next two sections, I will break down a couple of experiments that illustrate exactly how stereotype threat works. The devil is in the details. Exploring the details will allow us to put the problem of stereotype threat back into the big-picture viewpoint of a student's evolutionary biology – and the terrible conflicts that arise at school.

Casting Evil Spells

Take, for example, the stereotype of women being less mathy than men. In 2006, college women took a two-part math exam similar to the GRE (Nimrod and Heine, 2006). However, they were unaware of something tricky that lurked in a reading section sandwiched between two math sections. There were four different versions of the reading. One version described gender-differences in math performance, and declared that the reason women underperformed men was genetic. The next version claimed that women performed worse in math because of differences in experience. Another version stated that no difference existed between the sexes in math ability. The last version of the reading simply made the women aware of the fact that they were women, without mentioning math.

The results were surprising. Women who read that there was no gender difference, or that the difference was due to experience, both scored significantly higher. Those who read that math performance was genetic scored lower. Most interestingly, those who got the reading that simply made them aware that they were women had similar low scores. What a jinx! Simply by telling women that their math skills were innately inferior, or, by calling attention to their gender and allowing prevailing stereotypes to do their dirty work, the womens' math performance dropped. Our reputations are of such importance to us humans that a few words can vex us into bad grades. We should take a look inside and see what is going on.

A Look Inside: How stereotype threat works in the brain

A similar experiment on the effect of stereotype threat on female math performance was carried out, only this time, fMRI was used to actually see how stereotype affected activity in different areas of the brain (Wraga, et al, 2006). The women performed as previous research would have predicted. Women who faced a negative stereotype underperformed those who received a neutral statement. Additionally, women who received a positive stereotype significantly outperformed both groups.

In the case of the positive stereotype, the group of women were told that females had greater ability at taking multiple perspectives. The math test required the participants to imagine that they were rotating, a task that would require an 'outside perspective' of the body. In this clever way, the women were able to benefit from a prevalent positive stereotype about women that would also enhance spatial-mathematical thinking.

More interestingly, women who faced the negative stereotype revealed increased brain activity in the ventral anterior cingulate cortex (vACC) which is sensitive to negative social information. The vACC processes threats to a person's reputation, assessing the size and nature of the threat. In this experiment, the vACC area of the brain was so busy dealing with the stereotype threat, that it came at a detriment to areas of the brain involved in performing math (Wraga, et al, 2006). There is only so much processing power to go around; this diversion of very finite resources to the vACC part of the brain is a monkey on the back of the math problem-solving neurons.

This debilitating pattern of neural activity for women in mathematics has been confirmed in subsequent stereotype threat research using fMRI visualization (Krendl, et al, 2008). In these experiments, social-emotional processing areas of the brain took priority, shunting vital processing power away from math areas.

In contrast, the women who read a neutral statement showed brain activity mostly related to doing math, such as areas involved in calculations and spatial reasoning. They also lacked activity in the vACC, the part of the brain that assesses threats to reputation.

A positive stereotype allowed women to outscore groups

that read negative or neutral statements. Their fMRI results showed that they were able to focus the most cognitive resources to areas of the brain involved with math. The higher scores are a result of being able to efficiently use limited cognitive resources for the math problem-solving task at hand. This shows not only the limitations of the brain, but also the evolutionary priority our social status plays in academic endeavors.

Talking About My Reputation

The universality of the stereotype threat phenomenon indicates that there is a common mechanism to all of our brains that may be triggered. There is obviously something much older, deeper, and more personal going on here.

Whatever is causing a threat to our identities is provoking an ancient system that evolved to protect our reputation on the personal level, amongst people we already know. Let me provide an example. If a teenage girl's mom tells her she is 'lazy' or 'messy' with the orderliness of her room, the same part of her brain is impacted as when she hears negative stereotypes about women and math. The difference is that our brains have evolved to deal with this type of threat in a close knit hunter-gatherer society. That girl can take the negative feedback from her mom and assess the threat as being insignificant. After all, her mom usually complains about everything. She does pause to realize her room admittedly could use some picking up. The threat to her reputation has been mentally dealt with. She can now move on to making a mess somewhere else with a clear conscience.

However, in our 'less mathy girl' stereotype, a problem emerges. The brain structures that are adapted for managing her reputation amongst her friends and family in a hunter-gatherer-sized band are now forced to defend her reputation to nobody in particular and everybody in general.

Experimentation shows that the vACC is activated by

negative trait words that are perceived as personally relevant, 'lazy' or 'messy', for example, (Moran, et al, 2006 and Somerville, 2006) as well as by negative stereotypes that are relevant to a person's identity. How does a girl begin to assess a threat coming from society at large?

Reputation is of primary importance to our survival and it is an important part of our intrinsic nature (Emler, 1990, 1992). Our intellect is adapted for processing what other people think about us. The defense of one's reputation is too important to let go. It is more important than allowing her to devote her full cognitive resources to math problems. And the negative stereotype is not going away. There is an endless supply of the negative stereotype – and no individuals to address the issue with. That should keep her brain busy! Stereotype threat is not often framed in this evolutionary context: a conflict with society's negative stereotypes, evolutionary biology, and school design.

Interventions to Combat Stereotype Threat

What has been tried to solve the problem? As part of a robust study, California middle schoolers (Cohen, et al, 2006) were asked to affirm the values that were most important to them and write about them in a paragraph. It had a profound impact on their grades. As crazy as it sounds, this simple act resulted in a 40% reduction in the black achievement gap relative to white students in one term. African American students bumped up their GPA's by .25 points (Grade Point Average, out of 4.0 points). However, African American kids with the lowest grades increased their GPA's by .4 points. In a Scientific American article, Yong (2103) pointed out that this gain may seem small, but iteratively, these academic gains may capitalize on one another in the future.

The cumulative negative effects of chronic daily stress from stereotype threat are difficult to summate. However, stereotype threat is one of those invisible things in the academic environment that needs to be pulled out into plain sight. Perhaps by measuring the impact of interventions to combat stereotype threat, we can begin to estimate the true size of its malignancy. The numbers in the preceding paragraph were achieved over a single academic term with a simple intervention; they reveal a need to put a much bigger spotlight on this sorcery and to directly address the impairment.

When students' academic trajectories can be bent upward like that, it is not a stretch to realize that academic and even career trajectories are severely compromised by stereotype threat. The cumulative stress of a negative feedback cycle operating over years is evident in the discrepant outcomes of school achievement we see today. The results of studies like the one just mentioned above are helping to create stereotype threat interventions that are being scaled up for wider use (Yong, 2013).

The success of African American students and others in stereotype threat intervention studies also highlights a theme of this text. When there is a conflict with a crucial aspect of our evolutionary human biology, those at the bottom of the achievement gap make disproportionate gains when the problem is rectified. This is because their fundamental humanity has been affronted more than non-achievement gap populations.

Double-Edged Sword

While I just focused on the impact of stereotype threat on the performance of the student, it can impact teaching performance as well. Teachers may hold a fear of confirming a negative stereotype of being ineffective at teaching a bottom-of-the-achievement-gap demographic like low-income, black, or native kids. Teachers also have had to deal with the negative stereotype of being less intelligent and capable than other types of professionals. It is therefore in the best interest of not only students to negate psychological threats in the classroom, but also of teachers whose performance may increasingly be measured by those students' test scores. Students who are subject to the damage of negative academic stereotypes face double-jeopardy when the teacher's performance is hindered. While the sword cuts two ways, somehow it is the student who ends up taking all the damage in the end.

Solutions: Short-Circuiting Reputation Management

If we want to improve test scores for those at the bottom of the achievement gap, we need to combat the persistent threat of negative academic stereotypes. This threat is real; big brains are an adaptation for sociality, not academics. If there is a negative stereotype about your identity in relation to the class you are taking, the battle is on! Your character and competence are continually being demeaned to the community. As a human, this is a priority thing to deal with and set right.

So how can we get all of our students to have their cognitive gears available to excel at school work? Negative academic stereotypes are pervasive parasites that threaten our academic pursuits. The chronic stress of reputation defense inhibits learning and severely compromises academic outcomes as well as future quality of life. Are we caught in a trap? Do we wait for stereotypes to change? Or, how do we circumvent this problem?

Fortunately, researchers have developed some successful solutions that have been tried in the classroom. Current approaches (Yong, 2013) to mitigating stereotype threat include these proven strategies: (1) increasing students' sense of belonging at school, (2) cultivating a growth mindset, and (3) a values affirmation intervention. In addition to these strategies, which help to buffer the impact of stereotype threat, I will discuss a forth strategy: (4) Re-framing Curricula by their Evolutionary Roots. I would now like to interpret these stereotype threat mitigation strategies from an evolutionary point of view.

(1) Sense of Belonging: Human social group sizes reprise

A sense of belonging at school does not come easy for every student. Our schools are tailored for a relatively narrow demographic. As a result, achievement gaps can be interpreted as just how well various demographics actually 'belong' at school. Because school is inherently a social endeavor, social adversity can also be read as a sign that you do not belong. The small stuff of social interactions can have ripple effects that can cause widespread damage to health and academics. Research shows that improving a student's sense of belonging has a profound effect on performance. In a study of college freshman (Walton, et al, 2011), African American students halved the achievement gap (in GPA) over three years when they received a brief social-belonging intervention. The intervention simply explained that social adversity was typical and fleeting to students as they adjusted to the new college environment. These issues of belonging are not confined to new college students. They are also at work at the K-12 level.

Would we expect a strong sense of belonging to develop in an environment filled with anonymity and unknowns? Of course not. One way to help students feel like they belong is by creating structures that inherently facilitate this. Optimally, promoting students' sense of belonging occurs within the hierarchy of human social group sizes. I argue for a relationship-rich environment where students can be known on an individual basis without defaulting to stereotype. When every student is known by their individuality, for better or worse, they have a greater potential of being an integral part of the school community. This sense of belonging is difficult to create amongst a large group, unfamiliar with one another.

Creating a sense of belonging at school means more than just good social integration. It must also mean arming each student with a firm identity as a learner. However, building an inclusive academic identity is a challenge. Schools are indelibly stained by achievement gaps. Yet, within the cognitive group size, we can have the capacity to know students beyond a default stereotype in a more safe, trusting, and socially connected environment.

The problem is, society's stereotypes are still there. There is no use hiding a person with a negatively stereotyped identity amongst a smaller group. The prevailing stereotype in society can fly right through brick walls into any classroom and sting us. Any number of things could trigger a reaction to these stereotypes and affect performance. We must create a more resilient academic identity that renders negative academic stereotypes irrelevant. I will further address the problem later in this chapter.

Another magic feature of the hierarchy of human social group sizes comes into play when a new student enrolls at a school. Within this size structure, a remarkably rapid assimilation of the new student into the social and academic fabric of the school may occur. This is a boon to transitions and may benefit areas where students must switch schools more frequently (such as schools with military bases nearby, areas with seasonal agricultural labor, neighborhoods with many recent immigrants, or students in transitional housing situations). The discrete hierarchy of human social group sizes can be a catalyst to achieving a more rapid and authentic sense of belonging in school.

(2) Growth Mindset

Psychologists have recommended a personally powerful method of mitigating stereotype threats in the classroom (Yong, 2013). It is what Stanford psychologist Carol Dweck (2006) calls having the 'growth mindset' in her text *Mindset: The New Psychology of Success*. The growth mindset is one that embraces the concept that intelligence is something that can be developed, rather than a fixed asset you are born with. Her research has identified the growth mindset as the key ingredient to success in life pursuits such as school.

To summarize roughly, Dweck says that when people believe that intelligence can be developed, they embrace challenges and feedback, value the role of effort, and are more resilient to struggle. On the contrary, if you believe your academic abilities are a fixed trait, 'I just wasn't born with the math gene. My Mom didn't have the math gene either.', then you end up sensitive and stymied. Viewing academic abilities as fixed traits can be even more damaging to high achievers than it is to those who struggle. If you don't really give a rip about your academic achievement, your identity as a learner may be less impacted by psychological threats than competitive students at the top end. Regardless of a student's current skill level, the growth mindset offers the best path to progress.

The growth mindset works to mitigate stereotype threat by short-circuiting the reputation management response of the brain. With the growth mindset, there is no threat to your competence or character. There is no need to look like you know what you are doing or worry about being judged for not already being good at it. Having complete mastery of the task is not relevant to your reputation right now. The result is in the future; the skill growth comes from experience. The emphasis returns to the process of learning: the here and now and fun of figuring things out. The distracting social-processing that turns the vACC part of the brain into a hamster wheel is thereby de-bugged!

A powerful example of what a child with a growth mindset can do is told in the story of Ray Ewry. Before the 'white men can't jump' stereotype, there was likely a 'white boy confined to a wheelchair by paralysis from polio can't jump' stereotype. Doctors told Ray as a child that he might not ever walk again. Nonetheless, back in the summer of 1900, Ray Ewry jumped over a bar 1.65 meters high (a shave under 5 feet, 5 inches) from a standstill to claim the standing high jump world record. I can just imagine what would happen if I stood in front of my wife, and then instead of reaching out to give her a hug, I swung my arms up and tried to leap over her head. Ray Ewry bagged more Olympic gold medals than Olympic heroes of much greater notoriety. Ray Ewry's athletic feats rest in obscurity today, but his effort and growth in ability from paralysis to world record is one of the greatest Olympic athletic stories rarely told.

A journey of a thousand miles begins with one very first step. Perhaps Ray Ewry embodied the growth mindset in his journey from wheelchair to jumping world record. However, the growth mindset is not just the stuff of epic athletic fables; rather, it is the stuff of how to learn to speak Chinese or how to tackle algebra.

The fixed mindset is a psychological trap that can turn a student into their own worst enemy. When a student believes they were either born with a certain skill or not, rather than believing they can learn and grow, that student is defeated before they even try. A fixed mindset constantly exposes a student's reputation to threats. Failures turn out just as you predicted. Both 'I'm just not a math person' as well as the belief of 'I am already an expert at math' can both lead to walls being put up that inhibit growth. Consider the star athlete or brainiac student who struggles with something new and is reluctant to take feedback. In my work with highly capable teens, this was not an unusual scene. The fatal flaw in 'fixed mindset' thinking is that it disregards the brain's plasticity, its innate ability to learn through experience. With effort, we can all adapt, develop, and master new abilities, regardless of our starting place or predisposed interests. The growth mindset is the biological truth to which our learning abilities are fated. Let's not allow ourselves to get psyched out of this fact.

(3) Values Affirmation

Values affirmation (Cohen, et al, 2006) has been shown to be a general way to effectively alleviate the effects of stereotype threat. (See previous reference to this study earlier in this chapter, under *Interventions to Combat Stereotype Threat*). By affirming values of personal importance, students define their character at school in positive terms. Positive thought provides a feedback loop that promotes resilience in brain areas sensitive to stereotype. Values affirmation provides an impressive buffer to stereotype threat by empowering students in their own positive terms.

(4) Re-framing Curricula by their Evolutionary Roots

As long as we are still human, reputation management will always be at the forefront of our minds. We have interpreted the burden of stereotype threat from an evolutionary perspective: maintaining one's reputation amongst a small group. We have just discussed three proven methods (growth mindset, values affirmation, and a sense of belonging) used by educators to mitigate psychological threats.

Sometimes, the conflict emanates more directly from the subject content itself. Instead of enduring a constant battle to refute negative academic stereotypes, perhaps it is time to further undermine them. I propose that by grounding our academic subjects in their evolutionary roots, we might begin to shake our subjects of their baggage that provokes psychological threat in the first place.

The truth is, many subjects from science, to math, to language contain historical baggage that have kept them out of reach to many. By facing the sordid history of these core subjects, we can reframe them so that every student can envision themselves as a scientist, a writer, or a mathematician. This is necessary because, as we discussed, it is inherent intelligence that is arrested by the school system in achievement gap populations. I will discuss framing subjects in such a manner as to see the subject's utility and power in actions that all of us evolved to do day-in and day-out.

In the following subsections, I will dissect the three subjects traditionally assessed by standardized testing: (A) science, (B) math, and (C) language arts. I will discuss strategies for further undermining stereotype threat in these subjects. Through an evolutionary framework, we can see problems and solutions surrounding psychological threats at school.

(A) SCIENCE

Science & Stereotype Threat

Even if every word of science that is ever spoken from here on out is narrated by Neil deGrasse Tyson, science will still carry its stereotypes that impact performance and participation in it's various fields. Scientists are often stereotyped in the whitest shade of a disheveled Einstein's lab coat. Science itself is typically framed in a Euro-centric perspective that won't claim its universal and global heritage. In other words, ancient Greeks in togas started to philosophize about atoms and, the next thing you know, modern European scientific discoveries flourish until the present flying-killer-robot I-pocalypse.

In even worse cases, science has gone beyond excluding people of color and women to actually using them as unwilling subjects in scientific experiments. In the previous chapter, I described how curiosity killed the cat when it wasn't even the cat's own curiosity that got it killed.

During his first term in office, President Obama made an international apology for research orchestrated by leaders of the most prestigious medical institutions in the United States in the years following World War II. A government report aptly titled *Ethically Impossible* (2011) recounts bizarre and sadistic STD experiments using prisoners, prostitutes, and other vulnerable Guatemalans. In the matter-of-fact prose characteristic of a government report, *Ethically Impossible* exemplifies a historic yet ongoing tragedy: People of color and others with low-status have often been used as lab rats, rather than being given medical care or meaningful roles in research (or receiving its benefits). A significant amount of our scientific knowledge has come at this hidden and *Ethically Impossible* cost. This discriminatory pattern is even true of some of the research cited to support arguments in this text. How do we give science back to the people, despite science's notorious progression?

Taking Back Science – by Taking it Way, Way Back

The truth is, we are all scientists and always have been. Today, we may have access to more accumulated collective knowledge, but we have the same biological hardware caged in our craniums as our ancestors did 100,000 years ago. I propose that we re-frame science in a more inclusive and universal foundation. We will turn to the 'First People' for cues. Specifically, we look to the Khoesan language-speaking peoples of southern Africa. These various *San* tribes were traditionally Kalahari hunter-gatherers until recent generations.

The DNA of *San* people started diverging from other humans around 100,000 years ago (Schlebusch, et al, 2012). They are the most phonemically (phonemes are distinct sounds used to make words) and genetically diverse populations. For much of the ancient human past, we were all hunter-gatherers. It may surprise those who descend from Ireland or England to know that their genetics largely come from a remnant of hunter-gather peoples who survived the last ice age in the 'Basque refuge' and later migrated to the British Isles (Oppenheimer, 2006). Ancient hunter-gatherers have the same brains capable of the same things our brains do today. So what do the traditions of the First People have to show us about science?

San-sational Science Stories

South African Louis Liebenberg's text *The Art of Tracking: The Origin of Science* (1992) is more than just a mere metaphor for modern science. Liebenberg makes a detailed case that persistence hunting (as practiced by skilled *San* hunter-gathers of the central Kalahari) provides the evolutionary anthropological context for the basis of modern scientific thought and practice. Research programs to find the Higgs boson, for example, and research programs to determine the location of running meat, are indeed one in the same. The two are not just analogous, they both make use of the exact same mental processes – the original science. Let me further summarize Liebenberg's (1992) work.

Tracking animals requires a deep background knowledge of the environment, animal behavior, biology, and the marks animals leave behind. Creative hypothetico-deductive reasoning must be used to efficiently catch up to an animal or handle gaps in the signs. Tracks are interpreted by reading the mind of the animal, so as to successfully predict its next move. Many variables factor into how best to pursue the animal, including the hunter's own vitals. A hunter is prepared to be skeptical of another's hypothesis, and rigorous scientific debate may break out when conflicting interpretations of the animal signs occurs. Beyond the physical evidence, the credibility, experience level, and persuasiveness of the hunters may also weigh into the argument. Afterward, telling the story of the hunt contributes to the collective research program (Liebenberg, 1992). When we think less about the lab coat and more about the lifestyle, modern scientists should find these actions to be very familiar.

So here we are referring to a practice performed by every living human's ancestors. Each and every one of us, and all of our ancestral lineage going all the way back to the great-grandmother or great-grandfather common to both you and I and everybody else alive today, was good at practicing science and lived amongst a community of scientists who employed scientific culture daily. This is most certainly true or you and I wouldn't be alive, here and now. You can't take that pedigree away from anyone. How did we move from a world where everyone was a practicing scientist to a world where a paltry privileged percentage are deemed scientists? When we think of our scientific process skills, we can envision these iconic hunter-gatherer acts.

Science is a Verb

Science (verb) creates science (noun), which informs further science (verb). Science, in its verb form, is epitomized in the 2015 movie *The Martian*, when the astronaut played by actor Matt Damon proclaims *"I am going to have to science the shit out of this."* in his quest to survive abandoned on Mars. He uses his knowledge and creativity to plan, execute, and trouble-shoot his survival. Unfortunately, school science is much more of a noun than it is a verb. Let's further explore this verb '*to science*' in its traditional context.

Traditional *San* persistence hunters refer to their scientific hunting practice as the "Great Dance". *The Great Dance: A Hunter's Story* (2000) is also the title of a documentary by Craig and Damon Foster which documents some of the last !Xo San persistence hunters.) Science can be framed as this Great Dance.

In schools, the Great Dance has become the great list of Greek-derived vocabulary words. Education researchers emphasize that a spatial and motor orientation to science learning can benefit girls. Girls may capitalize on learning through sensual memory associated with doing science (Gurian & Stevens, 2004). Additionally, the movements of doing science provides resistance to psychological threat through several mechanisms affecting reputation-sensitive areas of the brain.

Persistence hunting epitomizes science as a verb – and a social, sensory-integrated verb at that. As we science, scientific culture becomes an inherently natural lifestyle for kids. The movements of science become fully engrained. Every kid out there already has research programs going on right now, you just might not know about them yet. Most even have collective research programs going on amongst their friends. My boys study ninja squirrels, among other things.

As we promote a future with greater equity in science achievement, let's remember the Great Dance. Science isn't a compilation of facts, or a process you start learning about in middle school. It is just what we do – it is the culture that came wired with our bipedal *Homo sapiens* hardware. Science will surely benefit from greater diversity if we want to address 21st century problems. Everyone should have an opportunity to benefit from lucrative STEM careers, just like we did 100,000 years ago. Returning science to its roots provides corrective action for universal success.

(B) MATH

Stereotype Threat and Mathematics

In 2005, then Harvard President Lawrence Summers drew outrage for remarks stating that women were under-represented in math and science fields due to "innate" differences. In doing so, Lawrence Summers, who has held some of the most prestigious and influential positions in academia and economics, invoked a stereotype threat condition applicable to women. While purportedly an academic discussion, his statements emboldened entrenched myths about women in mathematics and seemed to disregard a large body of evidence suggesting social factors may underlie this difference.

College women drop out of STEM fields at 150% the rate of comparably achieving college men after taking calculus due to lack of confidence (Kuo, 2016), so this is no trivial difference. In experiments, school-age girls show a small effect size for stereotype threat damage on STEM-related tests. (Flore & Wicherts, 2015). Brain imaging reveals that boys do tend to have some neurological advantages in spatial processing which is of some consequence to mathematics learning. Regardless, is there another biological truth in which we should frame the subjects of mathematics?

Who's Counting

The Lembobo Bone is a ~37,000 year-old baboon fibula from the mountains of Swaziland in the south-east of the African continent. This primate leg bone features 29 markings engraved on it. There is speculation that the markings could be interpreted as the number of days in a lunar calendar. There must have been a reason for its creation. Why was the precise length of a lunar cycle needed?

Humans have a hard-wired ability to estimate quantity, dubbed the *Number Sense* (Dahaene, 2001), to a precision of roughly ±20%. This is the math program we are born with – and it runs way, way back in our animal family tree. Being able to recognize how much is more is super important when it comes to food and survival. Adult humans, human babies, and even crows can visually distinguish which is the greater amount between 4 and 5; any closer ratio than that and 'more' gets fuzzily uncertain (Dahaene, 2011).

In creating a mathematical object that had specifically 29 markings, this human may have been in need of a precise count instead of knowing a lunar cycle as roughly what feels like 30 days, give or take a handful in either direction. In the *Universal Book of Mathematics*, author David Darling (2004) speculates that "...it may have been used as a lunar phase counter, in which case African women may have been the first mathematicians, because keeping track of menstrual cycles requires a lunar calendar." The Lembobo Bone shows the first documentation of our mathematical culture building upon that innate number sense foundation.

Our innate, number-line-like number sense is the evolutionary neurological truth that comes with our human hardware. Our powerful, flexible, and dynamic brains give us the ability to connect other neurons to this number sense infrastructure (Dahaene, 2001). This has helped to give rise to our amazing mathematical culture in all its forms and applications. So it turns out that math is something we cannot take away from anybody, regardless of ethnicity or gender.

The 'number sense' roots mathematics in a foundation that may help vanquish negative stereotypes. Framing coursework in such a way may further help to provide immunity to psychological threats.

* * I will note that the small percentage of students who have the most difficulty with math often have dyscalculia. In some forms of dyscalculia, students are 'blind' to numbers, reflecting problematic differences in the student's underlying 'number sense' circuits. Traditional approaches to math instruction may prove frustrating or even futile for such students, who must be identified early on and provided with appropriate interventions.

(C) LANGUAGE ARTS

Stereotype Threat and Language Arts

English Language Arts curricula consist of reading, writing, speaking, listening, and language. Boys face a significant achievement gap in language arts. In my home state of Washington, the gender-based literacy achievement gap mirrors national trends. The spread between the average scores of 8th grade girls and boys on the state's Language Arts assessment was 13.4% (2014-15 Smarter Balanced Assessment, which assesses Common Core standards: 63.8% of girls were able to meet the state's English Language Arts Standards, whereas 50.4% of boys passed the standards). For reference, an average (both genders) of 41.2% of low-income, 36.3% of black, and 31.6% of native 8th graders in Washington state met the English Language Arts Standards. So, some boys are substantially worse off than the average.

This gender achievement gap may be in part due to biological brain differences in boys that are thwarted by school culture (Gurian & Stevens, 2004).

> "With more cortical areas devoted to verbal functioning, sensual memory, sitting still, listening, tonality, and mental cross talk, the complexities of reading and writing come easier, on the whole, to the female brain."
>
> – (Gurian & Stevens, 2004)

Multiple experiments have confirmed that even young boys in kindergarten and primary grades are aware of overall negative stereotypes about boys' performance in school, especially in language arts. During experiments, this psychological threat condition inhibited boys' test scores in reading and writing (and math) (Hartley, et al, 2013). Because boys of this age may be subject to a stereotype threat in literacy and success at school in general, we have to acknowledge that this psychological threat may share some responsibility for this achievement gap. More importantly, how do we avoid a negative feedback loop, a self-fulfilling prophecy of lackluster literacy achievement? I will describe that there are indeed inconsistencies with juvenile male *Homo sapiens* biology with regards to literacy curricula. I will explain the problem and present a few solutions in the spirit of the evolutionary theme of this text.

English is Girly

The idea of a predominant 'girly' stereotype for English is more prominent than we might care to acknowledge. *"English is for Sissies"* is literally headline news in the island nation of Jamaica, and this case study can help us to expose the language achievement gap in a different light.

People view others as inherently more trustworthy when they share a common dialect (Dunbar, 1996). Boys have a natural tendency to retain their local dialects. In hard times, falling back on mom, family and the local community would have been an essential evolutionary strategy for survival. Females, on the other hand, may employ a different strategy called hypergamy. This involves having the ability to adapt to a more standardized or higher class dialect. Hypergamy would allow a woman to marry into a life of better opportunity and survival not only for herself, but her children as well. A brain that is more attuned to the nuances of language may make this integration easier. This sets up an inherent and invisible conflict in the classroom.

This principle can be seen at work today on the bilingual island of Jamaica where both Standard Jamaican English is spoken alongside Jamaican Patwa, which contains Akan influences. In 2015, US President Obama opened to a University of West Indies crowd with a rhetorical greeting of *"Wha a gwaan Jamaica?"* before he continued in Standard American English. Both languages have regular, predictable rules in use, but have disparate levels of privilege in society. The Jamaica Gleaner newspaper can often be read with direct quotes of citizens in Patwa and the surrounding report written in the standardized Jamaican English dialect.

A headline in the Sunday September 6th, 2015 edition of Jamaica's The Gleaner proclaimed *'English Is For Sissies!' - Crisis As Boys Rejecting English Language*. It stated that some boys view the standardized English as *"girlish"*, and a sign of *"effeminacy"*. Stereotypical girl traits, such as good behavior, including stillness and quietness, as well as the ability to grow literacy skills under such conditions, surely reinforce an *"English is for Sissies!"* point of view. English proficiency is perceived to be in a state of crisis on the island, and a widening gender achievement gap appears to have followed in-step with this rejection of standardized English.

> "Boys want to grow into men who are accomplished and responsible and professional and can earn money and please girls and all those things. What we need to get across to them is that the command of the English language is absolutely essential to do this."

> – Ronald Thwaites, Jamaican Minister of Education, as quoted in the Jamaica Gleaner, 6-Sep-2015.

We can find this same issue in schools around the globe. In Germany, regional dialects, some of which cannot be mutually understood, are more common amongst the lower and middle classes (Nees, 2000). Many of these Germans have learned a *'toned-down'* dialect, a more common and standardized version of High German, *Hochdeutsche Dialekte*. Schools play a standardizing role in language and result in eliminating local dialects. We could list countless examples, but we know that there are universal principles at work here.

Regardless of the privilege of standardized English in higher education and the ability to earn a good wage, there is a more primal evolutionary issue at work. Dialect is a deep matter of trust and survival. It is essential that educators understand this mystery, as it has the power to explain and predict patterns of disparate academic performance. This same pattern that affects lower class boys in school can be found globally.

Dialect inherently puts lower-income boys in a conflict. Their identities, trustworthiness, and reputations are being put on the line everyday in school by the nuances of dialect. Coupled with susceptibility to a negative language arts stereotype, this all amounts to a heap of trouble that might be way off the teacher's radar. What is the teacher's dialect, gender, class, etc.? What is the dialect of the reading material? How does this compare to the student? These are important and inherent matters of trust to a social brain. After all, that is why 'we' are sitting 'over here' in the cafeteria, and 'unnu' are sitting 'ovah dehso'.

A more cosmopolitan approach to language, in which local dialects are valued as equally legit (McRaven, 1966), and standard dialects are viewed as a common trade language, may help remedy this conflict. One way to accomplish this is by framing language arts by its evolutionary roots: our words are replicators in their own right – just like our genes.

Our languages are undergoing mutation / selection and random processes of their own. If a teen comes up with a novel way of saying something, as they often do, will this variation spread? Will it stick? Only time will tell. No matter how standard a standardized dialect becomes, it never stays still. Languages are constantly evolving and changing.

All of us, regardless of our dialect, are using language to fulfill a primal evolutionary function – coordinating and maintaining relationships amongst our families, friends, and neighbors. An understanding of the evolutionary nature of language, and its evolutionary purpose in humans, may help to circumvent stereotype threat in the language arts classroom.

Movement, Language, and Stereotype Threat

Movement is key not only in producing language and enabling literacy, but mitigating psychological threats to the language arts as well. Boys often face disciplinary consequences because of their need to link movement to language. How does the teacher's style accommodate movement during reading and writing instruction? Troubleshooting with human evolution in mind pulls all this invisible trouble into the light. These problems are easily short-circuited once they are identified.

As the father of boys, I know that young boys spend most of the day playing different versions of the same thing that I call OMTS: Objects Moving Through Space. It is not unusual to play six or more versions of Objects Moving Through Space before lunch. Examples include riding bikes, tossing balls, throwing paper planes, jumping off the steps, building Lego creations that end up flying and shooting, and throwing rocks in puddles (all in which, the mind's eye actually sees dinosaurs escaping cataclysmic meteors). Movement allows language to play to the spatial-processing and motor-wiring of boys, as well as many other complex benefits to language that arise from the simple accommodation of movement. I will argue how this is more than just a fun fact, but an essential part of literacy for boys.

Shakespeare as Opening-Act

In a clever data visualization, Matt Daniels (http://polygraph.co/vocaublary.html) plotted the number of unique vocabulary words in the first 35,000 lyrics of various Hip Hop artists and compared it to the first 35,000 words of seven Shakespeare plays (*Hamlet, Macbeth, Othello, Romeo and Juliet*, etc.). Whether the beat was boom-bap or iambic pentameter, with vocabulary as the parameter, a surprise emerges! Shakespeare fell on the plot at a nudge past the Beastie Boys, with 5170 unique words. Although acknowledged as the undisputed Don of the English language, Shakespeare's tongue fell far short of several Wu Tang Clan members.

Whether this mind-blowing data revelation makes you cringe or gets you excited about language, what is important is what we can deduce from these facts. I used a Hip Hop example here not so much to defy demographic stereotype – but to reiterate what happens with what Hip Hop emcee and philosopher KRS-ONE defines as "intelligent movement" (KRS-ONE, 2009). Hip Hop is all about movement. Recall when I argued that the benefits of movement are complex and multifaceted. Even walking has been shown to significantly increase language creativity and production (Oppezzo & Schwartz, 2014). While acknowledging that a successful rapper may be at the vanguard of the linguistically-skilled, we can appreciate how movement and creative linguistic mechanisms can work together to give rise to language achievement.

Using fMRI, brain images of freestyle rappers in action revealed that words are coming from a place "beyond volitional control". Words are bubbling up from the deep by their own free will – outside of conscious control. The brain images revealed that a "network linking motivation, language, affect and movement" are active during lyrical improvisation (Lie, et al, 2012). Let me reiterate that last sentence again: movement, motivation, feelings, and words – all connected together! Pedagogically speaking, this sounds like a winning recipe for improving language arts performance in boys.

Better yet, the early phases of a freestyle rhyme are unfiltered. They fly underneath the boss's radar. Executive control is bypassed by using an alternate (cingulate motor) brain-wiring mechanism that moves your mouth and makes words manifest. This drives innovation, as the brain quickly shifts back to areas under top-down executive control to fit the context of the verbal realities of the line. Writing from this flow state may especially help boys add richer detail, use a broader range of vocabulary, and exhibit greater verbal creativity. While motionless, quiet, and generally pained, a boy may not have the drive to thrive in the harsh environs of sedentary-school language land. But, with the literary game on its feet, Shakespeare might have to take a seat. Never underestimate the power of movement to affect language when we are dealing with a young, talking, bipedal primate!

Serotonin and Psychological Threat

Serotonin is a neurotransmitter implicated in mood, will-power, memory, attention, and learning. As you can decipher from that list, serotonin's effects are highly relevant to academic success. Boys have lower serotonin levels than girls (Gurian & Stevens, 2004), but movement can increase these lower levels.

Negative experiences at school can become another double jeopardy situation for struggling students bound to desks. Serotonin helps prevent the anterior cingulate cortex from spinning negative thoughts about school experiences (Roiser, et al, 2008). Without opportunities for movement, in other words, without the opportunities for serotonin production, the drive, focus, and capacity to learn are hampered, guaranteeing less instances of success. Additionally, that sensitive part of the brain that is susceptible to stereotype threat is missing the resilience offered by serotonin, and is also stuck spinning those accumulated bad school memories. A vicious negative feedback loop of academic depression ensues.

When we recall positive experiences, this also boosts serotonin levels (Roiser, et al, 2008). Positive nostalgic thought may also help drive language achievement by providing resistance to the negative experiences, and the psychological threat that those unsatisfactory language arts learning experiences feed into. So here, boys can boost literacy by capitalizing on higher serotonin levels brought forth by movement. The movement creates the proper neurological state for academic success. The positive feelings of success, and recalling the memories of these instances further boosts serotonin. Movement and good times can remedy the academically depressed state. This again highlights a double-negative factor that can pragmatically be reversed to be a double-positive one. Otherwise, we are stuck with disproportionately adverse consequences that we can measure every single year.

Language Arts Summary

In summary, a more cosmopolitan and movement-oriented approach to language can work hand-in-hand to mitigate psychological and biological barriers to language achievement in boys. Framing language in an evolutionary context helps to free it from bias.

Stereotype Threat In Summary

Childrens' reputations face many challenges, tricks, and traps at school due to reputation's evolutionary importance. A decent portion of achievement gaps can be accounted for by stereotype threats. Addressing stereotype threat with proven strategies is essential to eliminating them. Creating a sense of belonging, affirming values, and promoting a growth mindset are not just successful intervention strategies, but are deep themes for exploration of the school environment. This is especially true when done through the lens of human evolution. Re-framing curricula by their evolutionary roots may further negate the psychological threat associated with core subjects.

PART V

Re-entry

CHAPTER 13

Ancient Futures

Follow the Puget Sound coastline southwest from Tacoma, Washington and you will eventually find yourself staring up at the blue-gray exterior of The Steilacoom Tribal Cultural Center and Museum. *"Ancient Futures"* is the motto displayed on the exterior. I found myself staring up at this phrase while pondering the conclusion of this text. Ancient Futures sums it up precisely. But this is not the only place we will find this theme.

As I turn up my headphones, the theme of an *Ancient Future* is found again. This time, it's heard in the refrain of reggae music, known for both its universal messages as well as a distinctive human heartbeat-at-rest tempo that provides a direct connection to human biology. Popular Jamaican artist Protoje's album titled *"Ancient Future"* (2015) uses this phrase explicitly.

The sentiment of Ancient Futures appears again in the urban centers of New York and other cities around the world through Hip Hop, a UNESCO-recognized international culture.

Ancient Futures is a recurring theme – from Northwest Tribes to Reggae tunes to Hip Hop. Why? Why do we hear this chorus being broadcast from oppressed populations? Why is this quite literally the writing we find on the wall? At their heart, human rights are at the core of equity gaps, including at school. Hip Hop philosopher KRS-ONE (2013) once declared:

> "The education that we receive today is all about the destruction of the ancient hominid."

But the truth is, this ancient hominid is alive today. Little Homo Sapiens is living, breathing, and struggling to learn in a system that is out of sync with his biology.

Hip Hop's innate global currency underscores its power and adaptability as a universal pedagogical model, due to its embrace of essential hominid traits. Hip Hop allows local culture to be layered over a universal human template. In that same spirit, I propose that this Little Homo Sapiens-centric framework can be of similar universal utility. When a framework is deeply rooted in human biology, it should work great anywhere.

At school, a human rights agenda on achievement gaps cannot be pursued until we make schools designed for humans, - right? This text presents some of the human factors that disproportionately affect achievement gap populations when they are maligned. Life has always confronted young humans with substantial struggles to overcome; but throughout our evolutionary history, young humans were not asked to check their human super powers at the door.

Populations facing poverty, racism, or other oppressive circumstances have traditionally leveraged social group sizes, movement, language, and other essential human traits to deal with tough circumstances. Unfortunately, as I have outlined in this text, schools systematically hamper these fundamental human aspects. These factors can help to level the field when implemented correctly. These are the primal human powers that allow us to perform well on this spring's standardized test, as well as the ability to thrive over a lifetime.

School systems may be able to get by with sloppily designed schools when students are not stressed. However, a school system that has a student population under stress must embrace fundamental human traits and capitalize on them, or suffer disproportionately from conflicts with juvenile human biology.

Building a New Model

Every public school district in America has the same mission statement. It goes a little something like this:

"AAA School District provides academic success for every student; they will be life-long learners and good citizens in a diverse world."

It is the first part, the "for every student" part, that has school districts banging their heads against the wall.

If you add up all of the research I have provided in support of a human-evolution based framework (a quarter of a standard deviation improvement here, a tenth of a point there, and so on...) and turned it into a model, we would see a powerful pattern. We would see the pattern that I have provided evidence for throughout the text: disproportionate gains for achievement gap groups and steady upward growth for everybody else. "Success for every student" is a mission that is possible, if we design our system for such outcomes.

In this 'paleo' pedagogical model, each piece of the model has an impact in improving the education of Little Homo Sapiens. However, the true power of the model occurs when the full model is implemented and the rich and complex interactions between each piece can occur. Little Homo Sapiens performs best when she can integrate all of her species-defining super-powers. You can find many of the factors in this text quietly at work behind successful schools.

Fracking and Finances

The school population must be 'fracked'. The fractal dimension, the scaling ratio between natural human social groups sizes that I discussed in Chapters 2-5, should be used to group students at all levels.

In financial terms, the ratio of students to teachers is the leading driver of expenses in schools. Many may fret that my call for fracked schools, driven by sympathy group-sized classes, and cognitive group-sized administrative units are economically out-of-reach for many school systems' budgets. Many schools are facing class-size mandates that are already in the upper sympathy group range, especially in K-3 classes. Premium public charter schools are often funded (Baker, et al, 2012) at a level that allows for this size structure. Independent schools that forgo elitist opulence for fundamental, quality programs with lean administration can also offer such ideal class sizes - at close to public school expenditure rates. In short, fracking schools is a financially pragmatic leap with a compounding payout of benefits to reap.

Best Places for ACEs

In recent years, a great deal of attention has been given to Adverse Childhood Experiences (or Environments), or ACEs for short. Educators are particularly interested in learning how to mitigate the damage from such upbringings. I did not use the language of ACEs in this text. However, this 'paleo' model of school design creates an environment that offers the natural buffers, resilience, self-regulation, social-skill development, and interpersonal knowledge that theoretically would allow these students to succeed. The evolution-based philosophy of this model supports all achievement gap populations, regardless of the specifics. As the evidence I have presented suggests, these disadvantaged kids receive a disproportionate boost relative to their peers.

A Revolutionary and Evolutionary Model

As a new paleo-pedagogy is born, the framework calls for a new educational field and further inquiry organized along this line of evolutionary thought.

This text serves up an interwoven series of evolutionary-themed conceptual way-points. These way-points combine the best of scientific theory from a variety of disciplines with what is deeply true about education and humanity. They are guiding stars in the night sky of evolutionary biology-driven school success. The constellation that emerges (the curriculum), can only be fleshed out by the cultural preferences, the vision, and the learning needs of the local population. The constellation can have as many different manifestations as there are cultures (some may see a bear, others a frying pan, or even a clam), but all cultures must navigate by this same hard-wired fundamental human biology, this same shared set of astronomical way-points that are not going away any time soon.

Using human evolution as a guiding principle in the design of schooling is an idea whose time has come. We must seek comfort in and harness the power of our humanity in its most essential form in order to realize our education ideals. Let's put an evolution solution to work for the benefit of school children. While we have not even discussed what we are going to learn or how we are going to learn it yet, these things too can be addressed through a human evolutionary framework. *Nothing in education makes sense except in the light of evolution!*

References & Further Reading

Army, United States (1994) Pamphlet 10–1: Organization Of The United States Army. Department of the Army. Washington, DC, 14 June 1994.

Baker, BD, Libby, K, & Wiley, K (2012) Spending by the Major Charter Management Organizations: Comparing charter school and local public district financial resources in New York, Ohio, and Texas. Boulder, CO: National Education Policy Center. Retrieved [6 June 2014] from http://nepc.colorado.edu/publication/spending-major-charter.

Barros, RM, Silver, EJ & Stein, REK (2009) School recess and group classroom behavior. Pediatrics 123(2): 431–36.

Booth JN, et al (2013) Associations between objectively measured physical activity and academic attainment in adolescents from a UK cohort. Behavioral Journal of Sports Medicine 0: 1–7.

Bryant, Diane I (2008) Mathematics Intervention for First- and Second-Grade Students With Mathematics Difficulties. Remedial and Special Education 29: 1.

Campbell, MC & Tishkoff, SA (2010) The Evolution of Human Genetic and Phenotypic Variation in Africa. Current Biology 20(4), R166 – R173. DOI: http://dx.doi.org/10.1016/j.cub.2009.11.050

Carrell, Scott E, et al (2010) A's from Zzzz's? The Causal Effect of School Start Time on the Academic Achievement of Adolescents. American Economic Journal: Economic Policy 3 (August 2011): 62–81. http://www.aeaweb.org/articles.php doi=10.1257/pol.3.3.62

Carskadon, Mary (1990) Patterns of sleep and sleepiness in young adults. Pediatrician 17: 5-12.

Carskadon, Mary, et al (1998) Adolescent Sleep Patterns, Circadian Timing, and Sleepiness at a Transition to Early School Days. Sleep 21(8): 871-881.

Carskadon, MA, Vieira, C, & Acebo, C (1993) Association between puberty and delayed phase preference. Sleep 16(3): 258-262.

Center on Education Policy (2008) Instructional time in elementary schools: A closer look at changes for specific subjects. www.cep-dc.org/_data/in_0001/resources/live/InstructionalTimeFeb2008.pdf

Centers for Disease Control and Prevention (2010) The association between school–based physical activity, including physical education, and academic performance. Atlanta, GA: US Department of Health and Human Services.

Chang, FM, et al (1996) The world-wide distribution of allele frequencies at the human dopamine D4 receptor locus. Human Genetics 98(1): 91-101.

Cohen, Emma EA, et al (2010) Rowers' high: behavioural synchrony is correlated with elevated pain thresholds. Biology Letters 6: 106–108. doi:10.1098/rsbl.2009.0670

Cohen, Geoffrey, et al (2006) Reducing the Racial Achievement Gap: A Social-Psychological Intervention. Science 313:1307.

Cohen, GL, et al (2009) Recursive Processes in Self-Affirmation: Intervening to Close the Minority Achievement Gap. Science 324: 400–403.

Cohen, Juliana FW, et al (2016) Amount of Time to Eat Lunch Is Associated with Children's Selection and Consumption of School Meal Entrée, Fruits, Vegetables, and Milk. Journal of the Academy of Nutrition and Dietetics: 116:1; 123-128.

Adolescent Sleep Working Group, Committee on Adolescence, Council on School Health (2014) School Start Times for Adolescents. Pediatrics 134(3):642-649. DOI: 10.1542/peds.2014-1697

Crowley, Stephanie, et al (2014) A Longitudinal Assessment of Sleep Timing, Circadian Phase, and Phase Angle of Entrainment across Human Adolescence. PLoS One 9(11): e11219.

Dahaene, Stanislas (2009) Reading in the Brain: The Science and Evolution of a Human Invention. Viking, Penguin Group; New York, NY.

Dehaene, Stanislas (2001) Précis of The Number Sense. Mind & Language 16(1): 16–36.

Dahaene, Stanislas (2011) The Number Sense: How the Mind Creates Mathematics. Revised and Updated Edition Oxford University Press; New York, NY.

Daniels, Matt. The Largest Vocabulary in Hip Hop: Rappers, ranked by the number of unique words used in their lyrics. Polygraph http://poly-graph.co/vocabulary.html Accessed 2-Feb-2015

Darling, David (2004) The Universal Book of Mathematics: From Abracadabra to Zeno's Paradoxes. Wiley. ISBN 0471270474

Dar-Nimrod, Ilan & Heine, Steven (2006) Exposure to Scientific Theories Affects Women's Math Performance. Science 314:435.

Davis, B (2011) Mathematics teachers' subtle, complex disciplinary knowledge. Science 332: 1506-7.

Ding, Yuan-Chun, et al (2002) Evidence of positive selection acting at the human dopamine receptor D4 gene locus. PNAS 99: 313.

Dreborg, Susanne, et al (2008) Evolution of vertebrate opioid receptors. PNAS 105(40): 15487–15492. www.pnas.org/cgi/content/full/0805590105/DCSupplemental

Dornfeld, Ann/NPR (2012) Less Recess For Seattle Students. KUOW News, Seattle. 20 JUN 2012

Dunbar, RIM (1996) Grooming, gossip and the evolution of language. London: Faber and Faber.

Dunbar, RIM, NDC Duncan, and D Nettle (1995) Size and Structure of Freely Forming Conversational Groups. Human Nature 6: 67-78.

Dunbar, RIM (1992) Neocortex size as a constraint on group size in primates. Journal of Human Evolution 20: 469-493.

Dunbar, RIM (2003) The social brain: Mind, language, and society in evolutionary perspective. Annual Review of Anthropology 32:163-181.

Dunbar, RIM (2011) Social laughter is correlated with an elevated pain threshold. Proc. R. Soc. B :1-7. http://rspb.royalsocietypublishing.org doi:10.1098/rspb.2011.1373

Dunbar, RIM (1993) Coevolution of Group Size Neocortical size and Language in Humans. Behavioral and Brain Sciences 16: 681-735.

Dunbar, RIM, Duncan, NDC and Marriott, Anna (1997) Human Conversational Behavior. Human Nature 8(3): 231-246.

Dunbar, RIM, & Hill, RA (2003) Social Network Size in Humans. Human Nature 14(1): 53-72.

Dunbar, RIM (2004) Gossip in Evolutionary Perspective. Review of General Psychology 8(2): 100 –110.

Dunbar, Robin IM (1998) The Social Brain Hypothesis. Evolutionary Anthropology 6(5): 178-190.

Dunbar, Robin (2003) Evolution of the Social Brain. Science 302: 1160.

Dunbar, RIM, et al (2007) Evolution in the Social Brain. Science 317: 1344.

Dweck, Carol (2006) Mindset: The New Psychology of Success. Random House New York, NY.

Edwards, F (2011) "Early to Rise: The Effect of Daily Start Times on Academic Performance." Working Paper, University of Illinois at Urbana-Champaign.

Eisenberg, Dan TA, et al (2007) Examining impulsivity as an endophenotype using a behavioral approach: a DRD2 TaqI A and DRD4 48-bp VNTR association study. Behavioral and Brain Functions 3: 2.

Eisenberg, Dan TA (2008) Dopamine receptor genetic polymorphisms and body composition in undernourished pastoralists: An exploration of nutrition indices among nomadic and recently settled Ariaal men of northern Kenya. BMC Evolutionary Biology 8: 173.

Eisenberg, DT (2010) Assortative human pair-bonding for partner ancestry and allelic variation of the dopamine receptor D4 (DRD4) gene. Soc Cogn Affect Neurosci 5(2-3): 194-202.

Eisenberg, Dan & Campbell, Benjamin (2011) The Evolution of ADHD. Social Context Matters. San Francisco Medicine October 2011:21-22.

Ellenbogen JM, et al (2006) The role of sleep in declarative memory consolidation: passive, permissive, active or none? Current Opinion in Neurobiology 16:1-7.

Emler, N (1990) A Social Psychology of Reputation. European Review of Social Psychology 1:171-193.

Emdin, Christopher (2010) Affiliation and alienation: hip-hop, rap, and urban science education. Journal of Curriculum Studies, 42: 1, 1-25.

Emdin, Christopher (2010) Urban Science Education for the Hip Hop Generation: Essential Tools for the Urban Science Educator and Researcher. Sense Publishers.

Faraone SV, et al. (2005) Molecular genetics of attention-deficit/ hyperactivity disorder. Biol Psychiatry 57: 1313–1323.

Feinberg, M, et al (2012) The virtues of gossip: Reputational information sharing as prosocial behavior. Journal of Personality and Social Psychology 102(5): 1015-1030. DOI:10.1037/a0026650

Flore, PC & Wicherts, JM (2015) Does stereotype threat influence performance of girls in stereotyped domains? A meta-analysis. Journal of School Psychology 53:25–44.

Frank, MG, et al (2009) Mechanisms of Sleep-Dependent Consolidation of Cortical Plasticity. Neuron 61: 454-466.

Frank, Marcos G & Benington, Joel (2006) The Role of Sleep in Memory Consolidation and Brain Plasticity: Dream or Reality? The Neuroscientist 12(6): 1-12.

Fedewa, Alicia L & Ahn, Soyeon (2011) The Effects of Physical Activity and Physical Fitness on Children's Achievement and Cognitive Outcomes. Research Quarterly for Exercise and Sport 82(3): 521-535.

Geoffrey L. Cohen, et al (2006) Reducing the Racial Achievement Gap: A Social-Psychological Intervention. Science 313: 1307.

Gilman, David Alan & Antes, Richard L (1985) The Educational Effects of the Introduction of a State Supported Program of Smaller Classes. A Study of the First Year of Indiana's Project PRIME TIME and Its Effects on Test Results (1984-85). A Comprehensive Analysis. Indiana State University, Terre Haute School of Education. 1-15.

Gizer, IR, et al (2010) Candidate gene studies of ADHD: a meta-analytic review. Human Genetics 126(1): 51-90.

Grady, DL, et al (2003) High prevalence of rare dopamine receptor D4 alleles in children diagnosed with attention-deficit hyperactivity disorder. Molecular Psychiatry 8: 536–545.

Gurian, M, & Stevens, K (2004) With boys and girls in mind. Educational Leadership 62 (3): 21-26.

Hartley, BL & Sutton, RM (2013) A Stereotype Threat Account of Boys' Academic Underachievement. Child Development. 84: 1716–1733. doi: 10.1111/cdev.12079

Hinds, DA, et al (2005) Whole-genome patterns of common DNA variation in three human populations. Science 307: 1072–1079.

Jacob, BA & Rockoff, JE (2011) Organizing Schools to Improve Student Achievement: Start Times, Grade Configurations, and Teacher Assignments. Discussion Paper 2011-08

Jones, Michelle (2015) Women's Prison History: The undiscovered country. Perspectives in History. Feb 2015. https://www.historians.org/publications-and-directories/perspectives-on-history/february-2015/womens-prison-history#.VOZ21sxZbYM.twitter

Keyes, Katherine M (2015) The Great Sleep Recession: Changes in Sleep Duration Among US Adolescents, 1991–2012. Pediatrics 135(3): www.pediatrics.org/cgi/, doi/10.1542/peds.2014-2707.

DOI: 10.1542/peds.2014-2707

Kinzler, K, et al (2009) Accent Trumps Race In Guiding Children's Social Preferences. Social Cognition 27: 623–634.

Krendle, AC, et al (2008) The Negative Consequences of Threat. Psychological Science 19(2): 168-175.

KRS-ONE (2009) The Gospel of Hip Hop: The First Instrument, 1st edition. Powerhouse Books.

KRS-ONE, (2013) Interview recorded 21-Jun-2013 in Bern, Switzerland, preceding a performance. Published on 4-Oct-2013 on YouTube by Jonathon Gasana: https://www.youtube.com/watch?v=E0wEEL1Sxgg

Krueger, Alan B & Whitmore, Diane M (2000) The Effect Of Attending A Small Class In The Early Grades On College-Test Taking And Middle School Test Results: Evidence From Project STAR. NBER Working Paper Series. Working Paper 7656, http://www.nber.org/papers/w7656

Kuo, FE, et al (2004) A Potential Natural Treatment for Attention-Deficit/Hyperactivity Disorder: Evidence From a National Study. American Journal of Public Health, 94:1580-1586.

Kuo, Maggie (2016) Low math confiedence discourages females from pursuing STEM disciplines. 22-Jul-2016, Sciencemag.org DOI:10.1126/science.caredit.a1600110; http://www.sciencemag.org/careers/2016/07/low-math-confidence-discourages-female-students-pursuing-stem-disciplines

Kurzban, R, Tooby, J, & Cosmides, L (2001). Can race be erased? Coalitional computation and social categorization. Proc. Natl. Acad. Sci. U.S.A. 98: 15387–15392. doi:10.1073/pnas.251541498

Lewis, Debra (2005) Probing Performance Gaps. Science 308: 1871-1872.

Liebenberg, Louis (1990) The Art of Tracking: The Origin of Science. David Philip Publishers (Pty) Ltd: Cape Town.

Liebenberg, Louis (2006) Persistence Hunting by Modern Hunter-Gatherers. Current Anthropology 47(6): 1017-25.

Liu, S, et al (2012) Neural Correlates of Lyrical Improvisation: An fMRI Study of Freestyle Rap. Scientific Reports 2: 834. doi:10.1038/srep00834

Machin, AJ and Dunbar, RIM (2011) The brain opioid theory of social attachment: a review of the evidence. Behaviour 148(9-10): 985-1025.

Mahy, Caitlin EV et al (2014) How and Where: Theory-of-Mind in the Brain. Developmental Cognitive Neuroscience 9: 68–81.

Maquet, Pierre (2001) The Role of Sleep in Learning and Memory. Science 294: 1048-1052.

Matthews, LJ and Butler, PM (2011) Novelty-seeking DRD4 polymorphisms are associated with human migration distance out-of-Africa after controlling for neutral population gene structure. Am. J. Phys. Anthropol. 145: 382–389. doi: 10.1002/ajpa.21507

McDavid Raven I, Jr (1966) Dialect Study and English Education. New Trends in English Education: Selected Addresses Delivered at the Conference on English Education (4th, Carnegie Institute of Technology, March 31, April 1, 2, 1966). http://files.eric.ed.gov/fulltext/ED070101.pdf

Medina, John (2008) Brain Rules: 12 Principles for Surviving and Thriving at Work, Home, and School. Seattle: Pear Press, 2008.

Miyake, Akira, et al (2010) Reducing the Gender Achievement Gap in College Science: A Classroom Study of Values Affirmation. Science 330:1234-1237.

Mollison, Bill (1991) Global Gardener with Bill Mollison. (Part I: The Tropics). Bullfrog Films: DVD ISBN: 1-59458-423-0

Moran, et al (2006) Neuroanatomical Evidence for Distinct Cognitive and Affective Components of Self. Journal of Cognitive Neuroscience 18(9): 1586–1594.

Mosteller, Frederick (1995) The Tennessee Study of Class Size in the Early School Grades. The Future of Children; Critical Issues for Children and Youths 5(2): 113-127.

NCES (National Center for Education Statistics) (2006) Calories in, calories out: Food and exercise in public elementary schools, 2005. Table 12. http://nces.ed.gov/Pubs2006/nutrition/tables/tab12.asp. Table 13. http://nces.ed.gov/Pubs2006/nutrition/tables/tab13.asp

Nees, Greg (2000) Germany: unraveling an enigma. Intercultural Press: Yarmouth, Maine.

Oppenheimer, Stephen (2006) British Origins: the surprising origins of the Celts, Vikings and Anglo-Saxons. Carroll & Graf, New York.

Oppezzo, Marily & Schwartz, Daniel L (2014) Give Your Ideas Some Legs: The Positive Effect of Walking on Creative Thinking. Journal of Experimental Psychology: Learning, Memory, and Cognition, 40(4):1142–1152.

Pickrell, Joseph K, et al (2013) Ancient west Eurasian ancestry in southern and eastern Africa. PNAS 111(7): 2632-7.

Presidential Commission for the Study of Bioethical Issues (2011) "Ethically Impossible" STD Research in Guatemala from 1946-1948. Washington, DC; www.bioethics.gov

Ramirez, Gerardo & Beilock, Sian (2011) Writing About Testing Worries Boosts Exam Performance in the Classroom. Science 331: 211-213.

Rietveld MJ, et al (2004) Heritability of attention problems in children: longitudinal results from a study of twins, age 3 to 12. J Child Psychol Psychiatry 45(3): 577–588.

Rendell, L, et al (2010) Why Copy Others? Insights from the Social Learning Strategies Tournament. Science 328: 208.

Rockoff, JE & Lockwood, BB (2010) Stuck in the Middle: Impacts of Grade Configuration in Public Schools. Columbia Business School and NBER.

Roiser, JP, et al (2008) The effect of acute tryptophan depletion on the neural correlates of emotional processing in healthy volunteers. Neuropsychopharmacology 33(8):1992-2006. Epub 19-Sep-2007.

Rosenthal, BM (2011) 'Alarming' new test-score gap discovered in Seattle schools. The Seattle Times, 18-Dec-2011.

Schlebusch, Carina M, et al (2012) Genomic Variation in Seven Khoe-San Groups Reveals Adaptation and Complex African History. Science 338: 374-379. DOI: 10.1126/science.1227721

Schoenfeld, TJ (2013) Physical exercise prevents stress-induced activation of granule neurons and enhances local inhibitory mechanisms in the dentate gyrus. J Neurosci. 33(18):7770-7. doi:10.1523/JNEUROSCI.5352-12.2013.

Serre, D & Pääbo, S (2004) Evidence for gradients of human genetic diversity within and among continents. Genome Research 14: 1679-1685.

Shakeshaft, NG, et al (2013) Strong Genetic Influence on a UK Nationwide Test of Educational Achievement at the End of Compulsory Education at Age 16. PLoS ONE 8(12): e80341

Shultz, Susanne & Dunbar, RIM (2006) Both social and ecological factors predict ungulate brain size. Proc. R. Soc. B 273: 207-215.

Steele, Claude (2010) Whistling Vivaldi And Other Clues to How Stereotypes Affect Us, 1st ed. W.W. Norton & Company New York, NY.

Steele, CM & Aronson, JJ (1995) Stereotype Threat and the Intellectual Test Performance of African Americans. Pers Soc Psychol. 69(5): 797-811.

Sornette, Didier (1998) Discrete scale invariance and complex dimensions. Physics Reports 297: 239-270.

Somerville, Leah H, et al (2006) Anterior Cingulate Cortex Responds Differentially to Expectancy Violation and Social Rejection. Nature Neuroscience Volume 9(8): 1007-1008.

Tamir, Diana I & Mitchell, Jason P (2012) Disclosing information about the self is intrinsically rewarding. PNAS 109(21): 8038–8043.

Tatum, Beverly Daniel (1997) Why are all the Black kids sitting together in the cafeteria? and other conversations about race. New York: BasicBooks.

Tucker-Drob, EM & Bates, TC (2015) Large Cross-National Differences in Gene × Socioeconomic Status Interaction on Intelligence. Psychological Science: 1-12. doi:10.1177/0956797615612727

Tyler, William J, et al (2002) From Acquisition to Consolidation: On the Role of Brain-Derived Neurotrophic Factor Signaling in Hippocampal-Dependent Learning. Learning and Memory 9: 224-237.

Underwood, Emily (2013) Sleep: The Ultimate Brainwasher? AAAS Science Magazine Online: 17 Sep 2013 http://www.sciencemag.org/news/2013/10/sleep-ultimate-brainwasher

US Department of Health and Human Services, National Institutes of Health, National institute of Mental Health (2011) The Teen Brain: Still Under Construction. NIH Publication No. 11– 4929.

Vaynman, S, Ying, Z & Gomez-Pinilla, F (2004) Hippocampal BDNF mediates the efficacy of exercise on synaptic plasticity and cognition. European Journal of Neuroscience 20: 2580–2590.

Voorspoels, Wouter, et al (2014) Can Race Really be Erased? Frontiers in Psychology 5: Article 1035, 1-7.

Wadlington, E & Wadlington, P (2008) Helping Students With Mathematical Disabilities to Succeed. Preventing School Failure 53:1.

Walker, Matthew P (2005) A refined model of sleep and the time course of memory formation. Behavioral And Brain Sciences 28:51–104.

Walton, Gregory & Cohen, Geoffrey (2011) A Brief Social-Belonging Intervention Improves Academic and Health Outcomes of Minority Students. Science 331: 1447-1451.

Wang, E (2004) The Genetic Architecture of Selection at the Human Dopamine Receptor D4 (DRD4) Gene Locus. Am. J. Hum. Genet. 74: 931–944.

West, Martin R & Schwerdt, Guido (2012) The Middle-School Plunge. Education Next. Spring 2012: 63-68.

White House Task Force on Childhood Obesity (2010) Report to the President Solving The Problem Of Childhood Obesity Within A Generation.

Williams, Jonathan & Taylor, Eric (2006) The evolution of hyperactivity, impulsivity and cognitive diversity. J. R. Soc. Interface 3(8): 399–413. doi: 10.1098/rsif.2005.0102

Wilson-Harris, Nadine (2015) 'English Is For Sissies!' - Crisis As Boys Rejecting English Language. Jamaica Gleaner, Sunday, 6 September 2015.

Xie, Lulu, et al (2013) Sleep Drives Metabolite Clearance from the Adult Brain. Science 342: 373-377.

Yong, Ed (2013) Armor Against Prejudice. Scientific American. June 2013: 77-80.

Zhou, W-X, Sornette, D, Hill, RA & Dunbar, RIM (2005) Discrete hierarchical organization of social group sizes. Proc. R. Soc. B 272: 439-444.

Acknowledgments

Eternal gratitude to my wonderful wife Jessica for all of her support, encouragement, and assistance; I could not have completed this without you! A huge thanks to my Mom for all of the encouragement, feedback, and listening to my ideas. Thanks to Aunt Karen for her insights and suggestions. Thanks to all my friends for their positive support of this project and their useful recommendations. Thanks to all of the scientists, peoples and cultures, lab rats, and school systems whose work I referenced and am inspired by.

About the Author

Steven Welliever is a STEM subject teacher and former independent school director from the Pacific Northwest. Steven is passionate about education and will discuss school improvement non-stop. From his broad experience as an educator; from uptown, to downtown, to out-of-town, he has seen what works and what doesn't. His keen insights as a science-lover and natural systems-thinker provide a refreshing perspective on school reform. Steven lives in Olympia, Washington with his wife and two children. This is his first book.